Robert E.Lee

Dennis R Archambault

p 32   Lessons Lee learned from Scott in the imperialist
war against Mexico.
         1.   reconnaissance
         2.   flanking attack

       Lieutenant Ulysses S. Grant thought is own against
Mexico as the most vile

p 33   North & South against Mexico for more land - once
obtained, Statehood of California upset the strategic balance
of North & South

p 75   Lee attacks and begins to dictate war conditions

Robert E.Lee

Peter Earle

Saturday Review Press
New York

Designed and produced for George Weidenfeld and Nicolson Limited, London

Filmset and Printed Offset Litho in Great Britain by Cox & Wyman Ltd, London, Fakenham and Reading

ISBN 0–8415–0256–0
Library of Congress
Catalog No. 73–75722

Saturday Review Press,
201 Park Avenue South
New York, N.Y. 10003

Contents

Introduction

TO THE MILITARY STUDENT the American Civil War poses one of the most intriguing questions in the whole history of armed conflict – why did the Union take four and a half years to defeat the Confederacy? When eleven southern states seceded from the Union in 1861 and elected Jefferson Davis 'President of the Confederate States of America', nineteen northern states remained loyal. The population of the North was 18 million compared to nine million in the South. The Union controlled nine-tenths of the country's industrial resources, two-thirds of its railways, all of its Eastern seaboard and most of its mineral resources. The North had a considerable superiority in the primitive firearms of the day, the Confederate troops being for the most part equipped with old-fashioned smooth-bore weapons – some of them obsolete and ineffective flintlocks. The Southern States inherited only a little over three hundred of the thousand regular army officers – not surprisingly, as the enrolment of cadets at West Point, the American Military Academy, was based upon a quota from each state. During the war between one and two million men entered the fight on the Confederate side, two to three million on the Union side. Yet when, on 13 April 1861, the Confederates, under General Beauregard, began the war by attacking Fort Sumter in South Carolina, it was not until 9 April 1865 that they surrendered at Appomattox.

Part of the explanation undoubtedly lies, as Field Marshal Lord Montgomery has suggested in his *History of Warfare*, in the fact that 'the South was fighting to protect its way of life and its homes from the invaders, whereas the troops of the North were fighting only for an abstraction – the principle of the Union'. There were, of course, other reasons, the most obvious being that the war was, in its initial stages, essentially one of improvisation in which the North found it impossible to make its superiority count. The small regular army of 16,000 was completely unprepared for operations on a large scale, and the Northern commanders completely failed to grasp the principles governing the rapid expansion of military forces. Instead of using their regular units as a cadre, providing leaders, instructors and staffs for the influx of volunteers, they obstinately kept them intact, with the result that the experience and skill of professional officers was concentrated in a few regiments, while the great citizen army was for the most part indifferently trained and led. The South, on the other hand, made the most of those professional officers who elected to fight on their side.

Undoubtedly the most illustrious of these officers was Robert E. Lee, described by Lord Montgomery as 'possibly the best American military thinker and organizer of those days . . .' and by Winston Churchill, rather more colourfully, as 'one of the noblest Americans who ever lived, and one of the greatest captains in the history of war'. In this book, Peter Earle examines the career of this remarkable man against the background of the Civil War – or as some purists would prefer to call it, the War between the States. His account, although it does nothing to diminish the magic of Lee's reputation, falls some way short of the uncritical enthusiasm reflected in Churchill's evaluation. From more than one battle Lee emerges as something less than the perfect commander. Even at Chancellorsville, where he defeated an army twice the size of his own and which is generally regarded as his greatest triumph, the losses which he sustained were appalling – he lost nearly a fifth of his army – and he allowed the remnants of the Federal army under General Hooker to escape across the swollen Rappahannock river; and at Gettysburg his decisive defeat by the Northern forces was due in large measure to his tendency to leave too much to his corps commanders – it has been said that at Gettysburg the Confederate forces had, in effect, no Commander-in-Chief.

Whatever his qualities or defects as a military commander, Robert E. Lee became a national hero after his surrender at Appomattox, and his loyal support for the Union after the defeat of the Confederacy is reflected in a letter to a former captain in the Confederate navy in which he wrote that 'the allayment of passion, the dissipation of prejudice and the restoration of reason will alone enable the people of the country to acquire a true knowledge and form a correct judgment of the events of the past four years.' It is appropriate that beneath Robert E. Lee's bust in the Hall of Fame, there should be inscribed the words:

Duty then is the sublimest word in our language. Do your duty in all things. You cannot do more. You should never wish to do less.

1 A Gentleman from

Virginia

W HO WAS THE GREATEST HERO of the American Civil
War? Even many northerners would have to admit that
one man stands out from all the rest, that great soldier and
gentleman from Virginia, Robert E. Lee. Such an assessment
pinpoints the paradox of this terrible fratricidal contest. The
morals seem to be on one side and the heroes on the other, and
the heroes lost. Did the heroes make a mistake?

Surely we should support the North which seemed to have
the overwhelming moral right? What a terrible thing for the
world if the decadent slaveholders of the South with their
army of poor white retainers should have won. No, we must
stand behind the forces of progress – plain, decent, bible-
reading folk from Indiana and Massachusetts, boys in blue
ready to destroy for ever the pretensions of the southern
gentleman and that degrading institution which supported
his gentility.

But was it really as simple as that? As the armies of the
North slaughter and burn and the South continues to resist
we begin to feel that the war must have been about something
more than slavery. Certainly the southerners felt this. They
saw the war as a struggle for self-determination, a viewpoint
accepted and applauded by many outsiders. The middle of the
nineteenth century was a time of many wars of independence,
as 'nationalities' asserted themselves and struggled to free
themselves of their oppressors, and the South could readily
be seen as another Italy, fighting to throw off the threat of
Yankee imperialism. What then was the truth? Was the South
fighting for slavery – or for self-determination? Was the North
fighting for freedom – or for empire? It puzzled people then
and it still puzzles us today.

The South is so attractive. How well the Southern myth-
makers have done their job. It is so easy to forget the reality of
slavery, and see the war through the eyes of sentimental story-
tellers who portray it as a fight between beleaguered chivalry
and the forces of Mammon. How easily do we, armchair
soldiers and romantics, see ourselves looking across the
cotton fields as our neighbours ride in, so gallant, so chivalrous, to destroy in languid conversation the upstart impu-
dence of those damned Yankees. Surely there is no doubt that
this agrarian life, this ideal civilisation, is superior to that
dollar-grabbing materialism, that steam and sweat parody of
real life which is conquering our Northern neighbours? The
proof, if need be, will be in war. Then civilisation will be put

Colonel Robert E. Lee and his wife Mary;
companion portraits by William E. West,
1831. (Washington and Lee University)

to the test. How could an army of degraded wage-slaves do anything but run before the gallant Southerners, bred on the land and born in the saddle with a gun in their hand? What do young men from Georgia care about numbers? One Southerner can whip six Yankees, or is it seven? What are the guns of Pittsburg when matched against Southern courage? Carrying the flag so patriotically embroidered by the Southern belles, our sisters and our mothers, we ride onwards through the Carolinas to prove once and for all that gentlemen are superior to mechanics.

Two myths – one Southern, one Northern – both with that grain of truth that invites acceptance. The war did have something to do with slavery but it also had something to do with self-determination. The Southern army was certainly composed of some slaveholders and some poor whites, but mostly of yeomen-farmers who had never owned a slave and were never likely to. Some indeed were fighting to protect slavery, but most were fighting to protect their homes against what seemed an unwarranted invasion or else because they feared the censure of their neighbours if they did not fight. Many were driven to war by their womenfolk. As a Georgian lady put it, 'If the Southern men had not been willing to go I reckon they would have been made to go by the women.' Perhaps the majority fought because men love the thought of war, adventure, travel and excitement, and could have no idea of the appalling slaughter and misery that they were riding towards. The same was true of their Northern rivals. Excitement and bounty money drew them from their homes. A small minority may have been true Abolitionists fired with a passionate determination to free the slaves, but most had no interest in slavery and their only feelings towards the Negro were ones of aversion. Some were factory workers, many were German and Irish immigrants, but the great majority were farmers engaged in remarkably similar occupations to the yeomen from the South.

This then was just a war, brought about by bungling, blundering, misunderstanding and propaganda like most wars, fought for the most part by ordinary people who paid with their lives for the ill-digested rhetoric of idealists, North and South; a war which was more than usually unpleasant because it was a civil war; a war whose result was to save the Union at the cost of over six hundred thousand dead, the South ruined and three and a half million slaves freed to

Virginian scenery at Shannondale Springs. (Radio Times Hulton Picture Library)

16

Lee's birth room at Stratford Hall; a fitting scene for the birth of a Southern gentleman. (Robert E. Lee Memorial Foundation Inc., Stratford, Virginia)

enjoy the doubtful privilege of liberty in a nation which had neglected to make that liberty meaningful or effective. And yet there was a certain nobility in the war itself. If it was not quite the clash between good and evil that it appears at first sight it was still drama: a drama of courage and endurance in which the outnumbered Southerners have left for posterity a record of stubborn bravery rarely matched in the whole history of war.

Even if we reject all those myths of Southern civilisation so patiently constructed by historians and novelists in the 1920s and 30s, how could we ever view with anything but admiration and sadness those gallant men of the Army of Northern Virginia who held the whole weight of modern civilisation at bay for four long years? *With Lee in Virginia* was the title of one of Henty's great yarns. We are all with Lee in Virginia in our hearts, proud to fight under such a leader and forgetting our tattered uniforms, our miserable supplies of rotten pork and corn and the long trail of blood that marks our barefoot retreat before the legions of that butcher, Grant. We may well echo the sentiments of the war-weary Southern soldier who remarked after Lee's surrender at Appomattox Court House on 9 April 1865: 'Damn me if I ever love another country.' But even he would always remember with admiration and affection the noble, grey-haired man of fifty-eight who finally admitted defeat that day – General Robert E. Lee, the fighting soul of the South and in the words of Winston Churchill 'one of the noblest Americans who ever lived, and one of the greatest captains in the annals of war'.

Lee himself was to become a myth after Appomattox: a myth to sustain an image of American courage and indomitance set apart from the sordidness of Civil War. While the South was being stripped bare by the victorious Northerners Lee had already become a non-partisan American folk hero. Of course it was not possible to forget completely that this heroic man had been so misguided as to lead the forces of the rebellious South. But, this apart, he stood for all that was good in the war – skill at arms, courage, tenderness to defeated foes – and he was held up as an example to American manhood in the future. The fact that it took so long to defeat Lee means that we today, when we read his history, get the best of all worlds. There is time for our Southern heroes to delight us, but in the end our Northern ideals win.

Robert E. Lee was the epitome of that conservative American stereotype – the Southern gentleman. For there was a substance behind the myth of the Southern aristocracy. There really were men who dwelt 'in large and stately mansions, preferably white and with columns and Grecian entablature. Their estates were feudal baronies, their slaves quite too numerous to be counted, and their social life a thing of Old World splendour and delicacy.' Most of these men lived in Virginia, along the James River or in the Northern Neck – the strip of land between the Potomac and the Rappahannock which was to be so ransacked in the Civil War. They were the descendants of seventeenth-century English immigrants, some but not all from the lesser gentry, who had flourished in the New World by growing the noxious weed, tobacco, to calm the nerves of their stay-at-home countrymen. Those who succeeded through greater capital, luck or application, piled plantation on plantation and added slave to slave until they had resources sufficient to support what they considered to be the life-style of an eighteenth-century English country gentleman. They rode to hounds and indulged in politics, married into each other's families, dabbled in letters and the arts and ruled their less successful white compatriots by monopolising local government. Their lives were dominated by the intelligent pursuit of pleasure and by a code of morals which owed much to Renaissance Europe's idealisation of the medieval knight. Chivalry, the duel, outrageous courage and a sentimental worship of defenceless womankind were the hallmarks of this code, subtly changed as the times changed, but surviving into the nineteenth century as a combination of the Victorian gentleman and Sir Galahad. If there was an aristocracy in ante-bellum America it was these men – the Lees, the Carters, the Byrds – together with similar small groups in Charleston and New Orleans.

In the nineteenth century their political importance and their incomes were to decline, but their imagined life-style was to form an ideal which a new generation of rich planters might strive to imitate. As King Cotton spread his dominion from the sea-islands of Georgia to the Mississippi, the hard-faced, ambitious men who rose to the top in the struggle for land, slaves and wealth that the new staple offered sought in middle-age to temper their acquisitiveness with some of the graceful ways of the Virginian gentleman. But they had too little time. In little more than one generation the cotton kingdom of the Old South rose, matured and then died to be replaced by a world in which the values of Virginia had been lost for ever.

These values were the values of Robert E. Lee. His background was impeccable. His father was 'Light-Horse Harry' Lee, cavalry officer, hero of the War of Independence and friend of George Washington. His mother was Ann Carter, lovely daughter of the third generation of rich Carters, perhaps the most successful of all the plantation dynasties of Virginia. From such a background Lee should have been a planter in the tradition of the Carters and the Lees. Such indeed may well have been his ambition but fate ruled otherwise. For dashing Light-Horse Harry Lee not only had two elder sons by Ann; he also had children by a former marriage.

Robert E. Lee was the third son of his father's second marriage, to Ann Carter (right) daughter of a wealthy plantation family. By the time Robert was four, General Henry Lee (left) was driven by debts and scandal to exile in Barbados. (Washington and Lee University; Pennsylvania Academy of the Fine Arts)

Not that it made much difference to Robert's inheritance, for his father was an incurable and always unsuccessful speculator in land. Light-Horse Harry had gone through most of the money of the Lees, as well as the fortunes of his two wives, before their families stopped him and forced the debtor general to live on sufferance in houses and on money that belonged to his eldest son, another Harry, and his second wife. Worse was to come. In 1809 when Robert was two, his father, a former Governor of Virginia, was imprisoned in his own state for debt. Three years later, freed from jail, he was involved in a political brawl in Baltimore, beaten up and disfigured for life. In 1813 he left his native country for Barbados, still in debt, dishonoured and a pale shadow of his former heroic self.

Nor was Light-Horse Harry's self-imposed exile the end of the dishonour of the Lees. A debtor could at least remain a gentleman and Robert could still honour his father's memory, even if he saw little of him and was determined not to model himself in all respects on his behaviour. Far worse was the behaviour of his charming eldest half-brother Henry Lee,

21

who earned the soubriquet of 'Black-Horse Harry' after a scandal that made true Virginian gentlemen shudder in disgust. In 1820 when Robert was thirteen, Harry committed the unpardonable crime of seducing his wife's nineteen-year-old sister. His infatuation was disclosed to all when the girl, his ward as well as his sister-in-law, gave birth to a still-born child. Deserted by his wife and hounded by society, Harry in his folly gave Robert an example of what it meant not to be a gentleman which he was to remember for the rest of his life. Always fond of the society of pretty girls, Robert never gave rise to a breath of scandal about his private life.

It was against this background of comparative penury and dishonour that his long-suffering mother brought him up to be great and good; a Virginian gentleman, offspring of the first inauspicious union between the Carters and the Lees. The absence and later death of his father and the removal of his two elder full brothers, Smith and Carter, to the navy and Harvard respectively, meant that Robert found himself at an early age the man of the house, responsible for looking after his sick mother and his two sisters, catering on a thin budget and taking his boyish pleasures when and where he could. Home was the clan: the vast cousinage of the two great families, rooms in other people's plantation houses or for a while in a rented house in Alexandria, the small port and urban centre which served the needs of the planters and farmers of northern Virginia. Lee had the normal education of his class – he was still a Lee even if a poor one – but he would have to earn his own living: no easy-going plantation life for him.

Lee's predicament was not all that unusual for young Virginian gentlemen in the early nineteenth century. The bottom had fallen out of the tobacco market and much of the once rich tobacco land of the great plantations was now eroded and hopelessly unfertile. Some survived by engaging in a more scientific and diversified agriculture, but many others of the former great families now found themselves relatively poor. There were solutions of course: a rich heiress or more often emigration to the new cotton lands to the south and west. But here it was often found that the virtues of the Virginian were of little value in the aggressive, materialistic conditions of the cotton boom. Their grandfathers had had what it took to come out on top, but two generations of gentility had softened them. Judge Baldwin describes the plight of the Virginian in the 'flush times':

All the habits of his life, his taste, his associations, his education – everything, the trustingness of his disposition, his want of business qualifications, his sanguine temperament, all that was Virginian in him, made him the prey, if not of imposture, at least of unfortunate speculations. . . . There was one consolation – if the Virginian involved himself like a fool, he suffered himself to be sold out like a gentleman. . . . Accordingly they kept taverns and made a barter of hospitality, the only disagreeable part of which was receiving the money.

But this was one lesson Lee had learned from his father's experience and he was never tempted to join the exodus from his native state. All his life he was to show concern over money and on the few occasions when he did make investments he kept a very close and un-Virginian eye on them. Accordingly, since his mother had not sufficient cash to allow him to follow in brother Carter's footsteps and go to college, he chose the best career available to him and applied successfully to West Point which he entered in 1825 at the age of eighteen. A military career was the logical one for a poor Virginian, especially for the son of a hero of the War of Independence, and Robert was to find many Virginians among his class-mates at the military academy.

Peace-time soldiering in nineteenth-century America was hardly an exciting life. Lee, who did extremely well at West Point, entered the engineers, the most popular corps for successful cadets. All his life Lee was to continue his military education, reading widely in all pertaining to his profession, but his actual work, though varied and quite interesting, was not particularly martial. The engineers were employed not only to build and maintain specifically military installations such as coastal fortifications, but also to assist the Federal government in the enormous work of providing internal improvements as the vast flood of native Americans and

While Lee was a lieutenant in the Corps of Engineers stationed on Cockspur Island, he sketched this diamondback terrapin. (The Bettmann Archive)

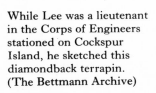

immigrants took up the empty lands across the Appalachians and pushed the frontier to the Mississippi and beyond. Lee's assignments varied from working on coastal forts in Savannah, Virginia and New York, to surveying unsettled territory in order to determine boundary disputes between new states. Perhaps his biggest job of all was that of clearing snags and altering the course of the Mississippi to save Saint Louis as a river port. Such work he always performed competently but it clearly gave no indication of his future military prowess. Promotion was slow and money was always fairly tight, especially after his marriage in 1831.

His bride was Mary Anne Randolph Custis, daughter of George Washington's adopted son, owner of the great house of Arlington across the river from Washington. Lee thus became in a sense the heir to the tradition of Washington, and it was this double heritage of the Washingtons and the Lees that was to insure the path he took thirty years later when the outbreak of the Civil War forced him to make the gravest decision of his life. Arlington was to become Lee's home when not on assignment, but marriage to Mary did not bring him wealth until her father died in 1857, and even then he had more trouble than luxury as executor of his eccentric and inefficient father-in-law's estate. Until then he had to support his wife and the seven children she bore him almost entirely on his army officer's pay.

Contemporary opinions of Lee during these formative years as a young and rather frustrated army officer are almost all complimentary. Indeed they tend to idealise him to a point where it is difficult to see him as a real man. Classically handsome, tall with a good figure, he made friends easily with young and old of both sexes, though he always kept a certain distance from complete intimacy. At an early age people were already using the adjective 'noble' to describe him and were remarking on his superiority to the common run of the human race. He never smoked, he never drank except the occasional glass of wine and he always kept his temper. But he was not a prig. His conversation was entertaining, he was sympathetic and kind, and he never sought to impose his taboos on others, an unusual self-denial in nineteenth-century America. He got on well with his subordinates in the army, combining discipline with friendliness in a manner likely to get uncomplaining good service out of them. He was tender to the weak, a good son to his mother whom he personally nursed through her

OPPOSITE A view of West Point on the Hudson River, where Lee took up his military career in 1825. Painting by Thomas Whittredge. (M. and M. Karolik Collection, Boston Museum of Fine Arts)

24

OPPOSITE At the age of twenty-four Lee married Mary Custis whose father owned the fine house of Arlington. The couple inherited the house in 1857. (Radio Times Hulton Picture Library; Custis Lee Mansion)

BELOW The formal parlour at Arlington. Over the fireplace is a portrait of Washington in the uniform of the Virginia militia. Mary Custis was the daughter of Washington's adopted son. (U.S. National Park Service)

The view of Washington
from Arlington House in
1836, by F.H.Lane. (I.N.
Phelps Stokes Collection,
New York Public Library)

final illness, a good husband to his not very attractive and
rather selfish wife and a good father to his numerous children.
As a colleague described him at the age of thirty-five: 'He was
quiet and dignified in manner, of cheerful disposition, always
pleasant and considerate, he seemed to me the perfect type of a
gentleman.' There seems no doubt that Lee would have been
happy with this description; a gentleman he wanted to be, and
that he was a perfect one is a tribute to his own self-discipline
and to that Virginian cousinage that produced him.

In 1846, at the age of thirty-nine, this model of virtue was
to get the chance to become famous. The occasion does not
seem to the historian to be particularly worthy, but then

28

Captain Lee had nothing to do with creating it. In May 1846
the United States Government invented an incident on the
Rio Grande as an excuse to invade Mexico and strip her of
some of her richest provinces. Lee's initial assignment in
this first major war fought by the United States since 1815
was purely as an engineer, but in January 1847 he was transferred to the force which the vainglorious general-in-chief
Winfield Scott was preparing to march from Vera Cruz to
Mexico City, in emulation of the feat of Cortez. Scott, a
fellow Virginian, had got to know Lee well some three years
previously, and impressed by his ability and his personality had
asked specifically for him to be transferred to his general staff.

29

The battle of Cerro Gordo, in which General Winfield Scott defeated the Mexicans, was Lee's first major engagement. (Radio Times Hulton Picture Library)

It was Lee's first chance to shine as a soldier and he made full use of it. He showed an almost instinctive talent for the feel of country and it was as a daring and imaginative reconnaissance officer that he made his name. On three major occasions between Vera Cruz and the final attack on Mexico City his reconnaissance of flank approaches through difficult and sometimes apparently impenetrable country, his construction of paths to take men and artillery into their flanking positions, his incredible powers of endurance and his bravery under fire brought him flattering mentions in reports, until the formerly obscure engineer captain became the best-known junior officer in the army.

Apart from gaining the reputation which was to ensure a high appointment when the Civil War broke out fourteen

years later, Lee had in the Mexican War his first and only
training in real warfare before taking field command of the
Confederate army in June 1862. This of course was just as
true of most of his regular army colleagues and opponents in
the Civil War, many of whom he met and fought with in the
Mexican campaign. What had Lee learned in the six months
he spent on General Scott's staff, six months in which he had
the privilege of seeing at first hand how battles were planned
and won? Was he given too much self-confidence by the ease
with which the poorly armed and poorly led Mexicans were
defeated? The confidence with which Lee as general led the
Confederate army into Union territory in 1862 and 1863,
despite enormous numerical inferiority, leads one to think
that Lee must have despised the Union generals as much as

Scott did the Mexicans when he cut himself off from his base in Vera Cruz to march on Mexico City. One reverse could have been fatal, just as Sharpsburg and Gettysburg might well have been fatal for Lee. There were other aspects of Scott's policy which may have been unwise examples for Lee to follow in the future. Was it wise, for instance, to admire so much Scott's habit of planning a battle and letting his subordinate generals work out the details of the plan on their own initiative? It was fine with a weak enemy or with generals who instinctively thought along the same lines as their commander-in-chief. But in the Civil War Lee constantly ran into trouble with this policy, especially with Longstreet who was far more cautious than he and whose slowness in getting into action jeopardised more than one of Lee's great battles.

Maybe Lee would have done better to have learned less from Scott, for what he learned by himself seems to have been in the long run more valuable. The most important lesson was the value of reconnaissance. This was Lee's great speciality and it is noticeable that at Gettysburg, his greatest disaster in the Civil War, he lost contact with his cavalry and for one of the few times in his military career had no idea where the enemy was. Another lesson was the value of the flanking attack. Lee's co-operation with his future great lieutenant Stonewall Jackson, whom he met in Mexico, was based very heavily on the surprise attack from the flank, nearly always the left flank – the same manoeuvre that he had reconnoitred and and advised so successfully in Mexico. Repetition of such a manoeuvre could well have been a mistake, though, as it turned out, each new left-flank attack seemed to come as a surprise to the Union generals.

When Lee rode in General Scott's victory parade through Mexico City in September 1847 he could look back with satisfaction on a successful introduction to the art of war. What he thought about the manifest imperialism which had brought about the war we do not know. The views of one of his younger colleagues, Lieutenant Ulysses S. Grant, have been recorded: 'I do not think there was ever a more wicked war than that waged by the United States on Mexico.' This 'wicked war', brought about largely by Southern expansionists and fought by an army in which Southerners predominated, was to have unforeseen results. By the peace treaty of 1848 Mexico recognised the United States' annexation of Texas and agreed also to cede to her imperious neighbour the territories of California, Arizona and New Mexico. Almost immediately gold was discovered in California and the mad rush of the 'forty-niners' across the continent began. In 1850 the swarm of white miners and settlers applied for the admittance of California to the Union as a free state. This had never been the intention of those Southerners who had advocated the war with Mexico. The delicate balance in the Union between free states and slave states had been broken and the long chain of events leading up to the thunder of Confederate guns firing on the Federal Fort Sumter in April 1861 had begun. California was to make clear to some Americans that their country was, in the future words of Abraham Lincoln, 'a house divided'.

2
A House Divided

W HILE THE NOW FAMOUS Colonel Robert E. Lee makes his way back from Mexico to the graceful portico of Arlington and reunion with his family, we must spend some time trying to discover what that awe-inspiring Republican lawyer from Illinois, Abraham Lincoln, meant when he described the United States as 'a house divided'. It is a confusing task, for the business of explaining the causes of the Civil War employs an enormous army of writers whose opinions are if anything more divided today than they were a hundred years ago. Indeed the quarrels of the past are still with us; North and South are still divided, and an opinion without sectional bias is almost impossible.

To the outsider the struggle seems to be about power and fear of what would happen when former power was lost. From an early stage in American history there was a clear distinction between North and South. Climate, institutions and culture were all different, though not as different as they were made out to be once sectional antagonism came to a head. The South had long hot summers, relied from an early stage on the great agricultural staples of tobacco, rice and indigo for the major part of her income, and started from the middle of the seventeenth century to depend increasingly on the labour of Negro slaves to produce these staple crops. Soon there developed a myth that these staple crops could only be grown with the labour of black slaves. No white man could survive the heat, the malaria and the back-breaking toil. This must have been patently untrue to anyone who knew the South at all. From early days these crops had been grown with white indentured labour, and all of the old staples together with the newcomer, cotton, were produced by white labour on white family farms right up to and beyond the Civil War. And few planters could honestly have said that Negroes were not susceptible to disease. The mortality of slaves from malaria and other fevers was so great that many estates, especially in the rice-growing regions, could hardly buy new slaves fast enough to replace the dead. Still the myth spread and the institution of plantation slavery became fixed in the South. It paid, and it enabled those who were successful to develop a leisured life which was envied both in the North and in the South by that great majority of white farmers and smallholders who had no slaves.

Life in the North was quite different. The weather was less friendly, soils were often poorer and agricultural conditions

PREVIOUS PAGES
Southerners dance on the Union flag at a wedding party. (Mary Evans Picture Library)

OPPOSITE Lee with his son Rooney. (The Virginian Historical Society)

36

were such that for the most part only those crops already grown in England and northern Europe could be produced. There was no advantage in large-scale plantations and the only profitable employment of Negroes was as house servants. Here then predominated small-scale family farmers working hard in an inclement climate to produce a bare subsistence or, if they were lucky, to produce a surplus for sale in the towns and ports that sprang up on the northern and central sea-board. For, unable to earn a good living by the production of tobacco or rice, enterprising Northerners turned to commerce and industry for their incomes. Great merchant houses flourished in ports such as Boston and New York, but although there were many rich there was less of that complete inequality so noticeable in the South.

On the basis of these economic and climatic differences a whole body of other distinctions grew up. Since so many of the New Englanders were descended from Puritan immigrants who had crossed the Atlantic in the first half of the seventeenth century, all Northerners were seen as puritans and had attributed to them the less endearing characteristics of that name. Northerners were misers, money-grabbers, philistine, un-smiling people who had lost the art of living. The Yankee, acquisitive and puritanical, was born. And if the Northerners were puritans then the Southerners must be descended from the English cavaliers: gay, chivalrous, generous, hospitable people, a fancy given some substance by the luxurious way of life being developed by some of the more successful planters in Virginia and South Carolina. Soon it could be argued that North and South, though descended from one common English stock, were really two different peoples.

Such apparent antagonisms were sunk in friendship during the struggle to free the colonies from the mother country and in the process by which the Republic and the Constitution were born. And indeed it seemed possible that the two halves of the new nation could co-exist for ever, since they were at this time fairly equal in political strength and neither could completely impose its will on the other. The ingenious system of checks and balances incorporated in the Constitution had seen to that, and the party system that grew up in the early nineteenth century was such that section was rarely set against section, each party drawing its strength from both regions.

But the march of events was to tilt the balance in favour of the North as the century went on. As the country filled up it

38

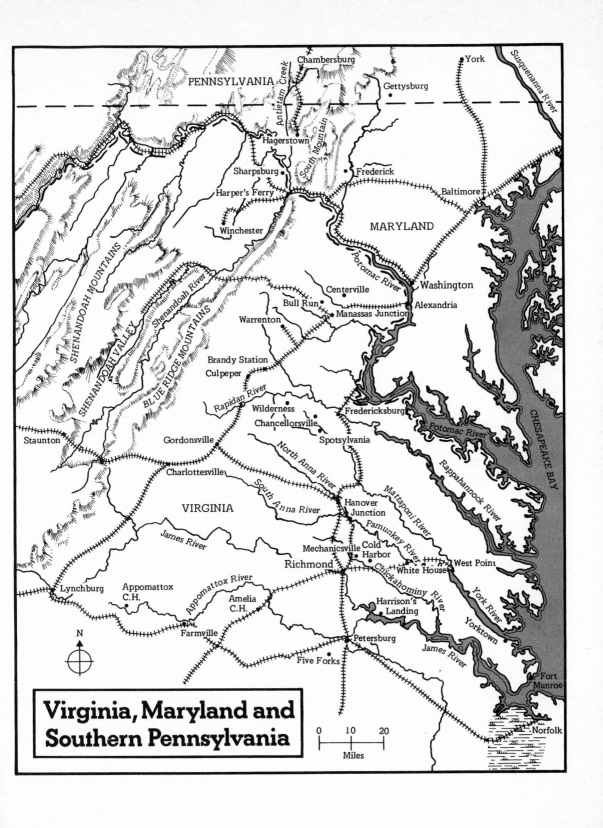

Virginia, Maryland and Southern Pennsylvania

PENNSYLVANIA

Chambersburg
York
Gettysburg
Susquehanna River

Antietam Creek
Hagerstown
South Mountain
Sharpsburg
Frederick
Harper's Ferry
Baltimore
Winchester
MARYLAND

SHENANDOAH MOUNTAINS
Potomac River
SHENANDOAH VALLEY
Shenandoah River
Centerville
Washington
Bull Run
Manassas Junction
Alexandria
Warrenton

BLUE RIDGE MOUNTAINS
Brandy Station
Culpeper
Rapidan River
Wilderness
Fredericksburg
Chancellorsville
Potomac River
Staunton
Gordonsville
Spotsylvania
CHESAPEAKE BAY

North Anna River
Charlottesville
Rappahannock River
VIRGINIA
South Anna River
Hanover Junction
Mattaponi River

James River
Pamunkey River
Mechanicsville
Cold Harbor
Richmond
White House
West Point
Lynchburg
Appomattox C.H.
Appomattox River
Chickahominy River
Amelia C.H.
York River
Harrison's Landing
Yorktown
Farmville
Petersburg
James River
Five Forks
Fort Munroe
Norfolk

N

0   10   20
Miles

was to the North that the great flood of white immigrants went, not wishing to compete with slave labour in the South. People from both sections crossed the Appalachian barrier and settlements spread to the Mississippi, but while in a spirit of compromise each new slave state was matched by a new free state, numbers – the basis of sectional strength in the House of Representatives – were clearly on the side of the North. This would hardly have mattered had not the institutions and the cultural patterns of the two sections been so different. Early on in the century many leaders of the South, especially those from South Carolina, had begun to evince a fear that one day the North would concentrate its political power in one party and use this strength to attack the institutions and way of life of the South.

Such fears were reinforced as the North began to industrialise and add to its numerical strength the power of big money. By the middle of the century many Southerners were convinced that the South was already an economic tributary of the North, and soon to be a political one as well. Ingenious calculations were made to estimate the tribute paid by South to North in the form of shipping freights, insurance, interest on debts, Southern taxation used for Northern benefits, payment for Northern industrial goods by the still agrarian South, and payments for holidays in the North by wealthy Southerners fleeing the heat that made their section what it was. Such calculations led to heated arguments over Northern demands for a tariff, seen by the South to be yet another form of tribute.

Fear of economic domination was reinforced by fear of cultural domination. Why did Southern boys go to Northern colleges to imbibe Northern, Yankee sentiments? Why were the school books used in South Carolina schools imported from Boston and stuffed with Bostonian sentiments? Surely Southern culture did not have to bow the neck to New England philistines? But, unfortunately, the much-vaunted Southern culture was composed almost entirely of a gift for oratory and good conversation. Art, literature and science were almost non-existent and indeed those who showed much originality in any of these fields were likely to be hounded out of Southern society by their reactionary fellows. The South imported and admired Sir Walter Scott and Carlyle, while the North produced all the original ideas.

This reinforcement of existing differences between the

sections produced two completely different societies, one bustling and economically aggressive, the other leisurely and rapidly falling further and further behind in economic terms. Two quotations from the marvellous diary of William Howard Russell, correspondent of the London *Times* who came to the United States in 1861 to report on the impending war, sum up the most obvious differences between the feel of the sections. 'New York', he writes, 'has certainly all the air of a *nouveau riche*. There is about it an utter absence of any appearance of a grandfather.' Later he dined at a planter's house in South Carolina, enjoying the claret mellowed in Carolinian suns and the Madeira brought cautiously downstairs from the cellar between the attic and the thatched roof. The conversation was as mellow as the wine and 'had altogether the tone which would have probably characterised the talk of a group of Tory Irish gentlemen over their wine some sixty years ago, and very pleasant it was'.

Pleasant it was and pleasant it might have remained had not the mellowness of South Carolina rested on the institution of slavery. This was the poison which was ultimately to kill the possibility of unity between the sections. The institution had been under attack since the eighteenth century and European anti-slavery sentiments had been echoed in America, both in the North and the South. But, despite individual opposition, slavery had been quite clearly written into the Constitution and the feeling that it might quietly die of its own accord had been shattered for ever by the enormous demand for cotton engendered by the English Industrial Revolution. Once it had been discovered that the fibre could be grown by slaves on plantations in the Deep South, there was little hope that slavery would ever die, unless enormous pressure was put on the slaveholders.

From the 1830s, as the cotton plantations and slavery spread to the Mississippi, the attacks redoubled and a strong minority voice for total abolition could be heard from the North. The vitriolic attacks of the Abolitionists were soon reinforced by attacks on every other institution of the South and on the supposed way of life of Southerners. A picture was painted of a degraded and debased aristocracy living in a state of total debauchery with harems full of black and mulatto concubines, maltreating and even sadistically murdering their starving black slaves. Few Abolitionists or Northerners had ever been to the South and much of what they wrote was

Slavery

The conviction that the Negroes were an inferior race permitted the Southerners to buy and sell them like cattle, often splitting up families. To escape the cruelty and repression of plantation life many Negroes fled to the North and to Canada by the 'underground railroad' helped by Northern sympathisers.

Not all the Southerners were tyrannical slave-owners. Many regarded their blacks in the sentimental light of 'A Virginny breakdown' (below), but even those who, like Lee, believed in eventual emancipation, would not accept that it should be forced upon the South by Northern radicals. (Virginia Museum of Fine Arts)

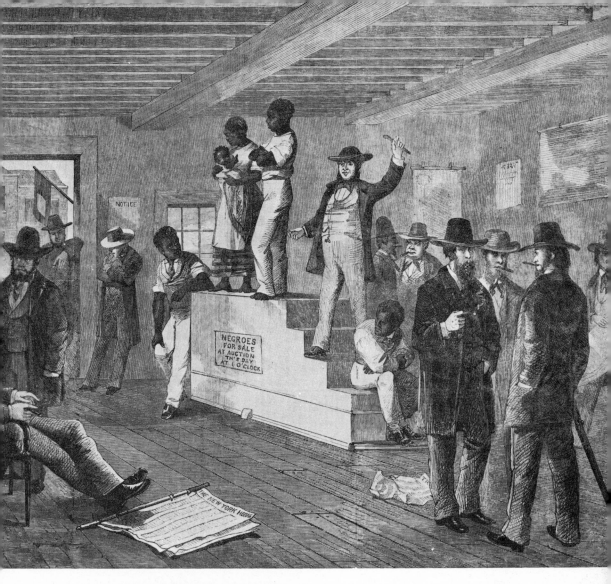

ABOVE A slave auction in Virginia, 1861.
(Radio Times Hulton Picture Library)

LEFT The slave market in Alexandria.
(Radio Times Hulton Picture Library)

pure fantasy or else generalisation from single instances, often gleaned from the law reports of Southern newspapers, but the campaign was ultimately only too successful in vilifying the South in the eyes of hard-working, but not necessarily over-moral, Northerners.

The first impulse of the South was to deny the stories, which for the most part were palpably untrue. But after the first flush of righteous indignation and apologetic literature the Southern writers changed their tactics and started to outdo Northern attacks in defence and praise of their institution. Abolitionist pamphlet was matched by pro-slavery pamphlet, novel by novel, until an equally fantastic picture of a happy South had been painted in which philanthropic slave-owners had created a new Garden of Eden for the poor, misguided, culturally deprived Africans. Listen to the moderate views of Edmund Rhett of South Carolina explaining the virtues of the Southern system to a stranger:

We are an agricultural people, pursuing our own system, and working out our own destiny, breeding up women and men with some other purpose than to make them vulgar, fanatical, cheating Yankees.... We have a system which enables us to reap the fruits of the earth by a race which we save from barbarism in restoring them to their real place in the world as labourers, whilst we are enabled to cultivate the arts, the graces, and accomplishments of life, to develop science, to apply ourselves to the duties of government, and to understand the affairs of the country.

Fraudulent anthropologists and geneticists were brought into service to prove that the African was of different descent from the white man, that slavery was the only possible exist-ence for him, that his brain was smaller and that what little he had consisted of less of the frontal portions, where intelligence was seated, and more of the rear where the animal emotions were. The Bible and the American Constitution were success-fully ransacked to provide support for slavery until all those in the Deep South who might have wavered in their attitude joined ranks in protection of the institution. Each side indeed believed or appeared to believe only its own propaganda in this war of words; there were few converts across sectional lines.

Despite the no doubt excellent intentions of the Abolition-ists, their attacks on slavery did little but harm. They never

44

offered any realistic solution to what seemed to that large body of Southern people interested in emancipation the most important problem – what to do with the slaves once they had been freed. The freed Negro fitted uneasily into the economic and social structure of the South, while in the North he met with as much, if not more, racial prejudice among the whites as he had ever met with in the South. For this reason alone the Abolitionists were acting in an irresponsible way. But the effects of their propaganda were to be far greater than simply to arouse a hate and disgust for Southerners in Northern eyes. By attacking the South they drew the section together in a common defensive attitude and in a common hate of Yankees and Abolitionists, words which had become virtually synonymous by 1850. To the fears of economic and cultural domination was now added a very real fear of political domination in which the slaves would be freed and all the institutions of the South pulled down.

This situation was feared not only by the planters but also by the farmers and poor whites who held no slaves at all. Writers in journals like *DeBow's Review* of New Orleans and orators all over the South told the non-slaveholders what would happen if the slaves were freed. Gone would be that caste line that gave them, even when poor, their status in Southern society; gone would be their protection against black competition for jobs and farms. The South would be full of insolent blacks ready now to insult them in their poverty and to rape their wives and daughters. They must stand shoulder to shoulder with the slaveholders to resist the North and the Abolitionists. If they weakened now their future would be one of race war and economic disaster. The non-slaveholders listened readily to such arguments and indeed, as events since the Civil War have shown, the poorer whites of the South have always held their interest to lie along colour rather than class lines.

Although one has to be careful not to exaggerate the fears of the South, especially during the crucial but prosperous years of the 1850s, it is against this background of mutual distrust and hate that events such as the entry of California into the Union as a free state must be seen. Anything which tended to tip the balance of political power further towards the North could be interpreted as the onset of disaster by the more radical, firebrand politicians of the South. There is no need for us to trace the road to secession in detail. Suffice it

to say that a series of blunders by politicians in both the North
and the South served to bring sectional passions to boiling
point as the 1850s went on.

Despite all blunders, however, compromise was still possible as long as political parties were not identical with sectional
interests. Up to the early 1850s potential Southern weakness
in numbers and economic power had not been matched by
actual political weakness. Southern politicians had more than
held their own amongst the leadership of both the great
national parties of the first half of the century, and had thus
ensured that sectional prejudice and sectional legislation was
kept to an acceptable minimum. The movement which made
secession inevitable was the formation of the Republican
Party in 1854. This alliance of a number of Northern political
groups – free-soilers, Abolitionists, xenophobes and New
England Whigs – adopted a fairly middle-of-the-road plat-
form. It had to if it was to win political power and still repre-
sent the divergent political views of its members. From the
point of view of Southern extremists, however, it was seen as
the very movement they had always feared. A sectional party,
existing only in the North, comprising supporters of the tariff,
abolition and the extension of free-soil states by giving land
away for nothing, could only be seen as a threat to the continued existence of the South as it then was. When Abraham
Lincoln was elected Republican President of the United
States in 1860, even though only on a minority vote, the game
was up. South Carolina, political leader of the South since the
1820s, seceded from the Union on 20 December 1860 to be
followed shortly by six other states of the Deep South. On
9 February 1861 they elected Jefferson Davis of Mississippi,
ex-soldier, slaveholder and a moderate by Southern standards,
the first President of the Confederate States of America.

So far we have talked about North and South as if there was
never any doubt which states belonged to which side, but in
fact there were eight states forming a solid barrier across the
country still undecided in their allegiance in early 1861. The
eighteenth-century boundary between North and South, or
to be more precise between slave and free, had been fixed by
Mason and Dixon's line, surveyed by two English astron-
omers 244 miles west from the Delaware River. Below this
line lay four slave states as yet uncommitted – Delaware,
Maryland, Virginia and North Carolina. Across the mountains were four more – Arkansas, Kentucky, Tennessee and

48

Missouri. The decisions of these states in the next few weeks would have a very important bearing on the outcome of the impending struggle. If they should remain neutral or support the Union with their military and industrial strength, there was little likelihood of the states of the lower South being able to resist armed pressure to return to the Union. But if they should decide to secede in support of their sister states to the South then the Union was indeed in danger. As it turned out they split exactly equally between North and South, thus ensuring that the Civil War would be the long and bloody struggle that it was.

The decision of no state was more important than that of Virginia. The most populous state in the South with a people of proven military talents, with good ports and almost the only industrial development south of the Potomac, Virginia could well swing the contest either way. Indeed it is not too fanciful to say that if Virginia had declared for the Union, or even stayed neutral, there would have been no war or at least it would have been a very short one, so great would Northern predominance then have been. And up to the very last moment it was uncertain which way Virginia would turn.

Virginia had seen many changes in the nineteenth century. Her great staple, tobacco, was in decline and as it declined the opportunities for profitable employment of slaves diminished in the state. A new economy was developing based on mixed farming and the encouragement of industry, similar to the economies of Maryland and Pennsylvania to the north. Many slave-owners had emigrated with their slaves to the cotton lands to the south and west, and many others had taken advantage of the high prices of slaves in these regions to sell their slaves out of the state. All these processes naturally diminished the feelings of common interest between those who remained in Virginia and the slave states to the south of her, while markets for her agricultural products increased her ties with the Northern sea-ports. Furthermore, of all the slave states, it was in Virginia that the strongest sentiment for the emancipation of the slaves on purely humanitarian grounds was to be found. Conservative and philanthropic Virginians supported the idea of transporting the freed slaves to Africa, and it was after a Virginian, President Monroe, that the capital of Liberia was named. Further support for the emancipationist movement came from the white non-slaveholding farmers of western Virginia, who were cut off by the mountains from

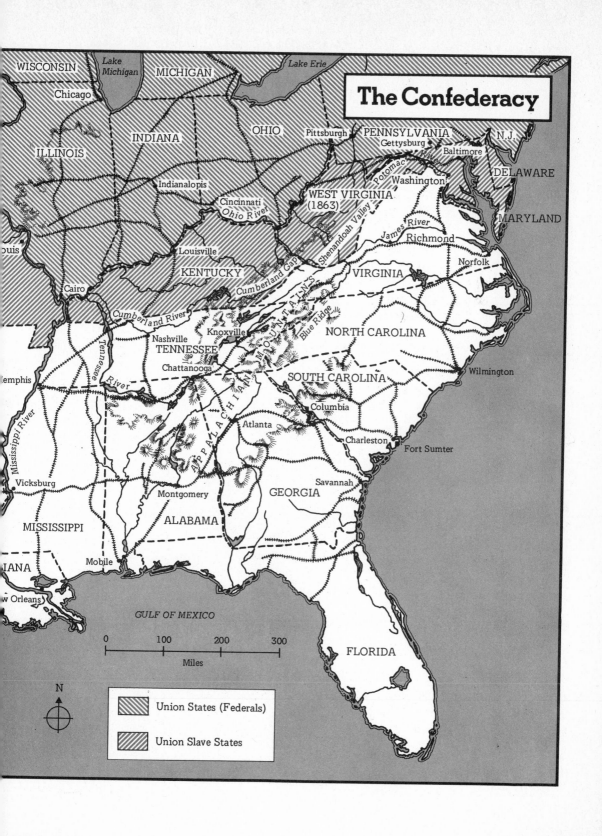

The Confederacy

WISCONSIN
Lake Michigan
MICHIGAN
Lake Erie
Chicago
INDIANA
OHIO
Pittsburgh
PENNSYLVANIA
Gettysburg
N.J.
ILLINOIS
Baltimore
Indianalopis
Cincinnati
Ohio River
WEST VIRGINIA (1863)
Potomac
Washington
DELAWARE
ouis
Louisville
James River
Richmond
MARYLAND
KENTUCKY
Cumberland Gap
Shenandoah Valley
VIRGINIA
Norfolk
Cairo
Cumberland River
Knoxville
Blue Ridge
NORTH CAROLINA
emphis
Nashville
TENNESSEE
MOUNTAINS
Chattanooga
SOUTH CAROLINA
Wilmington
Tennessee River
Columbia
Mississippi River
APPALACHIAN
Atlanta
Charleston
Fort Sumter
Vicksburg
Montgomery
Savannah
GEORGIA
MISSISSIPPI
ALABAMA
IANA
Mobile
w Orleans

GULF OF MEXICO

0   100   200   300
Miles

FLORIDA

N

Union States (Federals)

Union Slave States

The Confederate army storming a Federal stronghold during the early part of the war. (Andrew Mollo Collection)

much contact with Virginia proper and whose economy and ideas were far more in sympathy with the free states of Ohio and Pennsylvania. In 1831-2 a great debate had gone on in the state on the subject of emancipation and a motion to free the Virginian slaves over a period of time was only narrowly defeated.

It was therefore unfortunate that just at this time the attacks of the Abolitionists, not only on slavery but also on other Southern institutions of which Virginia was justly proud, should have had the effect of stiffening the resistance of the pro-slavery element in Virginian society, and of changing the

52

opinions of waverers from one of moderate anti-slavery to a rabid hatred of Yankees and Abolitionists, if not necessarily to extremist support of slavery itself. The events of the thirty years up to 1860 only served to strengthen the emotional identification of Virginians with the states to the south of them, at the same time as economic considerations were making slavery less important and tying the state more closely to the North.

Robert E. Lee was never a politician, but on the whole subject of slavery and the growth of sectional antagonism he reacted very much as one would expect a conservative Virginian gentleman to behave. He had little experience of slaves, except as domestic servants, until just before the Civil War and probably had no first-hand knowledge of the conditions of field-hands on cotton plantations in the Deep South. He lived among people who normally treated slaves well. Although he approved of eventual emancipation he considered that this should be a very gradual process. The following extract from a letter to his wife written in December 1856 gives a good idea of his views on slavery and on immediate emancipation:

The blacks are immeasurably better off here than in Africa, morally, socially, and physically. The painful discipline they are undergoing is necessary for their instruction as a race and, I hope, will prepare and lead them to better things. . . . Their emancipation will sooner result from a mild and melting influence than the storms and contests of fierce controversy.

It is clear that Lee, like most of his class, had been considerably affected by the pro-slavery propaganda of the past thirty years. It is doubtful if a man in his position would have written in quite such a conservative tone in 1830.

In the next three years Lee was to learn much more about both slaves and Abolitionists, but the experience probably did little to change his opinions. His father-in-law died in 1857 and Lee, who had had a variety of employments since the end of the Mexican War, including being Superintendent of West Point, asked for leave in order to settle his estate. The old man had left his affairs in chaos and Lee was forced to operate as a planter for two years in order to pay off the debts of the estate and the bequests in his will. In addition he faced the practical difficulties of emancipating his numerous slaves in accordance

53

with the requirements of the will. Lee undertook the task in his usual efficient way, but the experience only underlined the problem of emancipation. First-hand knowledge of plantation life convinced him that slavery had made the Negro unfit for continuous work, either as a slave or a freed man, so what was likely to be the effect of a general emancipation? Lee's planting activities aroused comment in the North, and he became much embittered by the unfair attacks of radical newspapers who took the opportunity to attack such a prominent member of such a prominent family by pillorying him as Colonel Lee, the brutal slave-owner who beats his slaves within sight of the nation's capital.

In October 1859 Lee got an even closer look at Abolitionists. A small group of extremists, led by the bearded fanatic John Brown and his brothers, had descended on the Federal arsenal at Harper's Ferry in northern Virginia to try to stir up a slave rebellion. Lee received orders to command the forces directed to resist them. When he arrived, he learned that the gang had been driven out of the arsenal by the local militia and were holed up in an engine house with a number of hostages. An offer to surrender was refused and Lee ordered a squad of marines to rush the doors. The capture and later hanging of John Brown was to be one more step on the road to Civil War. Nothing was more likely to make Virginia close its ranks than the fear of a slave rebellion; nothing could excite Northern Abolitionists more than a bearded martyr. John Brown's body was handed over to justice by Colonel Lee, but his soul was to go marching on through Georgia and the Carolinas until slavery was abolished and the South destroyed.

Lee was back in command of a regiment in Texas when the states of the lower South seceded. Recalled to Washington, he had time on the way to reflect where his future duty lay. He was never in doubt. Opposed to secession though he was, he was a Virginian before he was an American. If Virginia stood by the Union so would he. But if she seceded he would follow his native state with his sword and if need be with his life. Not all men in the border states took such a passive view. But to Lee it was unthinkable for a man of his name to fight against Virginia or indeed against any state of the South. This, too, was the view of his state's General Assembly which voted in February 1861 against secession, but also by a huge majority against the use of force to coerce the lower South. The ball

54

was therefore in Lincoln's court. If he used force he would have Virginia and others of the border states against him; if he did not, the Union would be lost for good and the seven states of the lower South would have succeeded in their unilateral declaration of independence.

Lee had to endure several weeks of growing tension as others made the decisions which would force him to do his duty for Virginia. Washington was in turmoil. Would Lincoln attempt to reinforce the Federal garrison at Fort Sumter in Charleston Harbour? Most of the other Federal forts in the lower South had been seized by the Confederates, but Sumter stood as a constant reminder of Federal unwillingness to accept secession. At last on 12 April the Confederate commander at Charleston, the stocky French creole General Beauregard, opened fire on the fort and made Lincoln's mind up for him. Two days later Fort Sumter surrendered to the 'hero of the South'. The following day Lincoln called for 75,000 volunteers to suppress the combination that was threatening the Union. All states, including Virginia, were required to furnish a quota to this force. The Civil War had started.

General Winfield Scott, Lee's former commander in Mexico and a fellow Virginian, was to make one last effort to secure the services of his distinguished subordinate for the Union. On his advice Lee was offered the command of Lincoln's 75,000 men. It must have been a tempting offer for a career soldier, but Lee's mind had been made up weeks before. 'Though opposed to secession and deprecating war,' he said, 'I could take no part in an invasion of the Southern states.' Sadly he left Washington for Arlington where he heard that the Virginia Convention had now voted two to one for secession. Lee sat down and wrote out his resignation from the United States Army. Then, saying what he knew was to be a long farewell to his home in Arlington, now directly in the path of invasion, he left for Richmond where his presence had been requested by Governor Letcher. One week after being offered command of the Union army he was offered and accepted command of the military and naval forces of his native state. His mother Virginia had placed her sword in his hand.

Lee's immediate task was formidable. He had to organise the training and arming of the host of inexperienced and hopelessly unrealistic militiamen and volunteers who sprang

OPPOSITE The people of Charleston watching from their housetops as Confederate forces under Beauregard open fire on Fort Sumter. (Library of Congress)

56

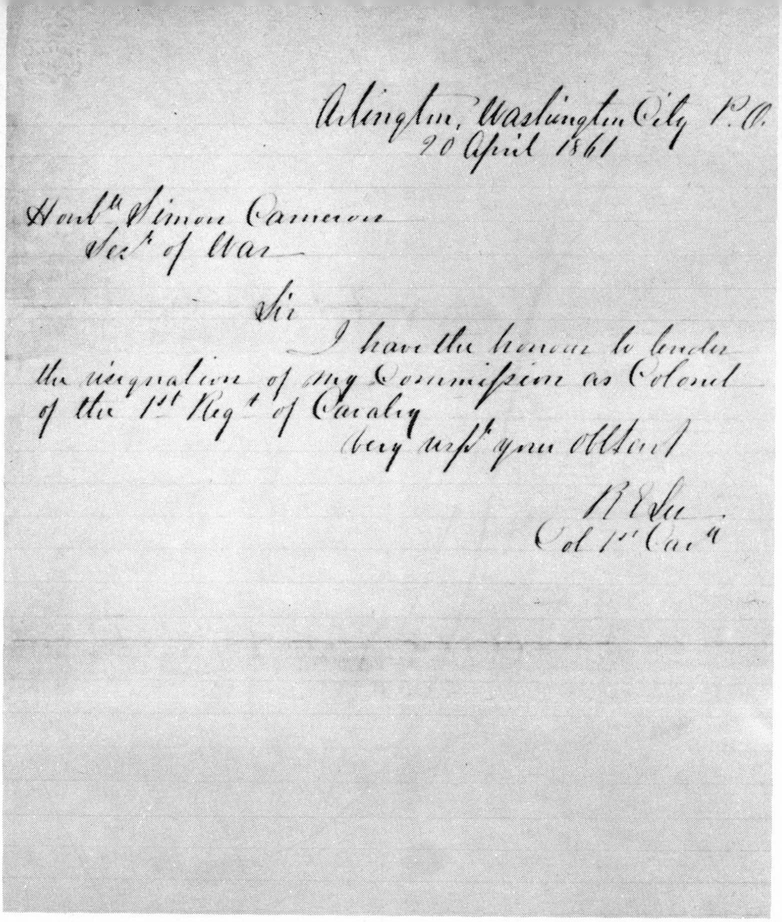

Arlington, Washington City P.O.
20 April 1861

Honble Simon Cameron
Secy of War

Sir

I have the honour to tender the resignation of my Commission as Colonel of the 1st Regt of Cavalry

Very respy your Obdt Servt

R E Lee
Col 1st Cavy

Lee's letter of resignation from the U.S. Army, 20 April 1861. (The National Archives of the United States)

forward to defend their state. Time was at a premium as Northern preparations gathered momentum, but Lee received valued assistance from other Virginian regular officers who rode home to offer their services. Soon units from other states of the South were moving north, for Richmond had been chosen as the capital of the Confederacy, despite its proximity to Washington, and it was clear that the defence of Virginia must be the first aim of the Confederate army.

The state was vulnerable from many directions. In the east many rivers, easily accessible to Federal forces sailing down Chesapeake Bay, led into the heart of Virginia. In the north, the Federal commander McDowell had already crossed the Potomac with what the *Richmond Examiner* described as 'the band of thieves, robbers and assassins, in the pay of Abraham Lincoln, commonly known as the United States Army'. He occupied Alexandria and made Lee's former home at Arlington his headquarters. Farther west, beyond the Blue Ridge, the valley of the Shenandoah, Virginia's bread-basket, was vulnerable to invasion from the Federal arsenal at Harper's Ferry, at the junction of the Shenandoah and the

Potomac. Lee had ordered the seizure of the arms and the arms-making machinery from the arsenal, but the place itself was too exposed to hold. Finally, in the very west of the state, beyond the main ridge of the Alleghanies, the situation was already hopeless. Here in the north-western counties of Virginia ties were much closer with the free states than they had ever been with the Tidewater. Unionist sentiment was very strong and the war had not been long under way before West Virginia itself seceded from the mother state to be formally admitted to the Union as a separate state in 1863. Meanwhile the central Shenandoah Valley was threatened by attacks across the mountains.

Lee demonstrated remarkable abilities as an administrator and co-ordinator as he struggled to put the state in readiness to defend itself. Badgered on all sides by firebrands who thought an immediate invasion of the North would end the war in a

The Federal munitions factory at Harper's Ferry. (Harper's Ferry National Historical Park)

few days, abused by gentlemen volunteers who objected to military discipline, he kept his head and prepared for what he expected to be a long struggle. In seven weeks he had created an armed force of 40,000 men. The coastal defences were strengthened and the rivers blocked to prevent their use by Federal gun-boats. The main Confederate forces were massed in the north at the important railway centre of Manassas Junction and in the lower Shenandoah Valley. But Lee himself was not in command. Jefferson Davis, a former professional soldier and Secretary of War, was determined to keep all military decision-making in his own hand. He kept Lee as his adviser at Richmond while command in the field was given to the popular hero, Beauregard, and to Lee's old friend and class-mate from West Point, Joe Johnston.

It was, then, at his desk in Richmond that Lee got the news of the first great battle of the American Civil War, the First Battle of Bull Run, a tributary of the Potomac to the north of Manassas Junction. This hard fight, in which the regular officers on both sides had great difficulty in controlling their green troops, ended in the panic flight of McDowell's Federal army back across the Potomac. Popular opinion forgot the desk-bound General Lee in the exultation at the great victory and Beauregard, Johnston and Jackson, who earned his soubriquet Stonewall at this battle, were the heroes of the Confederacy. Lee's reputation took a further knock in September when the newspapers accused him of timidity in not recapturing West Virginia for the Confederacy. Davis had sent him to the mountains to co-ordinate the efforts of a number of poorly led forces who were attempting to resist the advance of the Federal general McClellan. But co-ordination with no authority of command was a hopeless task. Lee prevented McClellan breaking through to the Shenandoah Valley but he could do nothing to recover West Virginia. The hero of Mexico returned to Richmond for the first winter of the war with the unfair label of 'Granny' Lee.

Joe Johnston and Beauregard, happy to have won the battle, made no attempt to follow up the Federal fiasco at Bull Run and the Unionists were able to reorganise their forces after this initial disaster. Lincoln, yielding to popular opinion, relieved McDowell of command and gave the job to the powerfully built, handsome General McClellan who had become the 'Young Napoleon' for his successes in western Virginia. McClellan's strategy was not as glamorous

60

RIGHT Jefferson Davis and the Southern generals. (West Point Museum Collections, U.S. Military Academy)

BELOW A Confederate detachment at Camp Corinth, Mississippi, 1862. (Andrew Mollo Collection)

George B. McClellan, whose
early successes in West
Virginia earned him the
nickname 'Young Napoleon'.
He was popular with his
soldiers for the care he took
of them but was no match
for Lee's daring strategy.
(The Bettmann Archive)

as his appearance, and as the months went by and no advance into the Confederacy was made, a rumble of disapproval could be heard. But McClellan knew what he was doing. He had decided that Richmond was the key to the Confederacy and that the way to Richmond was to use Federal naval power to land a massive army on the peninsula which lay between the James and York Rivers. Slowly he built his Army of the Potomac into a formidable, well-equipped and well-drilled force and at the beginning of April 1862 blue-uniformed soldiers began to land at Fortress Monroe, a bridgehead still in Federal hands at the tip of the peninsula. At Washington's insistence one large corps under McDowell was left on the Potomac to protect the capital and other troops were left opposite the isolated detachment of Stonewall Jackson in the Shenandoah Valley. Joe Johnston, not sure from which direction the Federal invasion would come, had withdrawn the main Confederate army to Fredericksburg on the Rappahannock River from where he would be able to use his interior lines of communication to oppose a move from either point. The peninsula itself was defended by the *bon viveur* general 'Prince John' Magruder who had already earned his laurels by the repulse of a Federal landing party in the early months of the war. It is estimated that the number of troops under McClellan's command was about twice those available for the defence of Richmond.

McClellan made his way up the peninsula, painstakingly and with the minimum of risk. Capturing Yorktown after a month's siege, he gradually pushed Magruder back towards Richmond. Johnston equally leisurely moved the bulk of his army across to face McClellan but seemed in no hurry to fight. The truth was that McClellan was now a very formidable opponent. Under cover of his heavy guns, which he was able to bring up the York River and then by railway from West Point, his force of some 100,000 men was able to take position after position. To attack him with the still comparatively green troops in Johnston's command would have been an extremely hazardous business. Meanwhile, Richmond was in turmoil as the less martial of the city's inhabitants made haste to get out before the apparently unstoppable Federal army should overwhelm them. The euphoria of Bull Run had disappeared. Davis himself, with whom Joe Johnston was on the worst of terms, was given virtually no information from his commander in the field and had no idea whether Johnston even intended to defend the Confederate capital.

Lee, as so often happened in this first year of the war, found himself in an absurd position. As adviser to Davis and an old friend of Johnston, he was almost the only channel of communication between administration and army, but even he found it difficult to get much sense out of his touchy, cautious old class-mate. He had no doubt that Richmond must be defended. The loss of the capital would have an appalling effect on Confederate morale, already shattered by the news of the capture of New Orleans by the Federal navy in April. Richmond was also the most important manufacturing city in the South and a vital supplier of arms and ammunition to the Confederacy. Lee could do nothing to control Johnston's operations in the peninsula except offer

The high street of Richmond in the early years of the war. Defence of Richmond was a prime consideration in Lee's manoeuvres and the Confederacy was to fall within a few days of the town. (Radio Times Hulton Picture Library)

advice, but he could use his ill-defined powers to create a diversion which might prevent the threatened junction between McDowell's corps on the Potomac and McClellan's invading force. Without consulting Johnston he instructed a number of scattered units to link up with Jackson in the Shenandoah Valley, thus giving this stern Presbyterian warrior the chance to demonstrate that mobility and aggression so shortly to be brilliantly employed by Lee himself. Jackson's famous Valley Campaign, in which he tied down four Federal generals at odds of three to one, so scared Washington that McDowell was never permitted to move south to aid McClellan in his attack on Richmond.

By the end of May McClellan had advanced to the line of the swampy, swollen Chickahominy River and his leading corps under Porter was at Mechanicsville, some six miles north-east of Richmond across the river, ready to link with McDowell if only Washington and Jackson would let him come south. It was at this point that fate appeared to play into the hands of the Confederates and give some hope that Richmond might yet be saved. McClellan had moved two corps of some 35,000 men on the left of his army across the Chickahominy to threaten Richmond from the east. But on the night of 30 May a Confederate god sent a storm which flooded the river, temporarily cutting McClellan's army in two. It was a chance which even Johnston, now with numerical superiority, could not miss. The next day he attacked the two isolated corps at Seven Pines. Lee and Davis, who had been given no information about Johnston's plans, rode out to watch the battle.

What little they were able to see was sufficient to show them that the battle had been very badly organised. The co-ordination between the Confederate commanders was very poor and this good chance of a convincing victory was frittered away in a hard-fought but indecisive battle. Johnston himself, at Davis's approach, rode off into battle without telling his President what was happening. Ironically, this instance of Johnston's antipathy to Davis served the Confederacy the best turn they had had since the war began. For Johnston was severely wounded and Davis had no real option but to offer Lee command. At last, over a year from the beginning of the war, Robert E. Lee was to leave his desk for the battlefield. The fate of Richmond was now to be left in the hands of Granny Lee.

ABOVE Lee on his horse Traveller attended by his aides. (Berry-Hill Galleries, New York)

BELOW Troop transport on the Nashville and Chattanooga Railroad. (Anne S.K. Brown Military Collection)

65

3
Seven Days Around Richmond

ROBERT E. LEE WAS FIFTY-FIVE years old when the accident of Joe Johnston's wound gave him his first experience of command in the field. Shortly after taking command he described himself in a delightful letter to his daughter-in-law Charlotte.

My coat is of gray, of the regulation style and pattern, and my pants of dark blue, as is also prescribed, partly hid by my long boots. I have the same handsome hat which surmounts my gray head (the latter is not prescribed in the regulations) and shields my ugly face, which is masked by a white beard as stiff and wiry as the teeth of a card.

Few people would have agreed with the general's description of himself. He was still outstandingly good-looking, very calm and rather reserved, but the sort of man who instinctively commands obedience and respect. Later he was to win the love of his troops as well, but at the moment his actual competence as a soldier remained to be put to the test. A rather hostile opinion of Lee by the indefatigable Southern diarist, Mary Boykin Chesnut, was possibly shared by many civilians in the South. Comparing him with his sailor brother Smith Lee she wrote: 'All the same, I like Smith Lee better, and I like his looks, too. I know Smith Lee well. Can anybody say they know his brother? I doubt it. He looks so cold, quiet and grand.'

Lee remained a family man first and foremost and it was to his family, particularly his wife and daughters, that he showed what lay behind the grandeur and the apparent coldness. His letters to his family often give much more insight into his real feelings about the fortunes of the Confederate cause, as well as showing a man who could banter and tease in a delightfully light-hearted way. A man with so many worries and responsibilities was still able to joke about his daughter's cat Tom, left at the enemy headquarters at Arlington. What strange things Tom must have learned. Perhaps a flag of truce should be sent in to find out how he is. As Lee moves around Virginia he describes the countryside and speculates on the harvest, always regaling his refugee family with the latest gossip about old friends amongst whom 'Cupid is very active'. Running through all his letters, personal and official, is continuous evidence of Lee's simple piety and belief in God.

Lee's family were a worry and a responsibility as well as a

LEFT A contemporary sketch of 'the rebel General, Robert E. Lee'. (British Museum)

PREVIOUS PAGES A Norther field hospital at Savage's Station, captured by the Confederates during the battle of the Seven Days in June 1862. (Library of Congress)

The uniforms of the
Confederate army. They
were little more than rags
by the end of the war.
(British Museum)

solace in the trying times of war. Mary his wife had been crippled by arthritis since the Mexican War and suffered increasing pain. After being compelled to leave Arlington she had lived a refugee existence for some months before settling in her son Rooney's home, the White House. Alas, this house, conveniently situated on McClellan's invasion route, was the second Lee home to be taken over by the enemy as a base. For a while after McClellan's invasion Lee lost touch with his wife, but then Little Mac, one of the most chivalrous and least vindictive of the Union generals, arranged for her to be escorted through the Federal lines so that she might be reunited with her husband. Rooney, Lee's second son, caused problems of his own. An enormous young man, 'too big to be a man and not big enough to be a horse', he was a reckless and very successful cavalry commander in his father's army, later to be captured by the Federals. But then what man with three sons and four daughters has no problems when commanding a rebel army in a civil war?

Lee's immediate problem was to turn the army he had taken over from Johnston into an effective fighting unit and save Richmond. Once he had done that he could turn his eyes towards the Union and try to justify the fighting name he had given to his command – the Army of Northern Virginia. He had few worries about the courage and stamina of the Confederate soldier. Bull Run and Jackson's Valley Campaign had given convincing evidence of Southern ability to defeat much larger armies. But several weeks retreating before McClellan had not done much to improve morale and Lee found much bickering and dissatisfaction in the army he took over. Discipline indeed was always the greatest problem of the Confederate army, a problem which paradoxically arose from its greatest strength. What one Englishman described as the 'swashbuckler bravado, the gallant-swaggering air of the Southern man' produced soldiers who would face certain death with a smile on their face, but were unwilling to submit themselves to orders from men whom they considered no better than themselves. Such an attitude was compounded by the Confederate policy of allowing the soldiers to elect their own officers. A popular officer was very often the most easy-going, and many a strict disciplinarian found himself returned to the ranks by the votes of his former command. Lee was able to tighten up discipline in the ranks, but was unwilling to be too harsh since maximum effectiveness depended on a combination of Southern individuality and regular army authority. Where Lee showed his greatest weakness was in his attitude to senior officers. He was always suggesting, rather than giving firm orders, and although such a friendly relationship worked on most occasions it sometimes led to disaster.

Later in the war Lee was to have appalling difficulty in supplying his army. The Confederate administration and the Confederate railway system were hopelessly inefficient and the soldiers suffered terrible deficiencies in food, clothing and transport. But while the army was so close to Richmond this was not too serious a problem. The men were well enough fed and though few of them wore the regulation uniform as laid down by the authorities they were at least decently clad, the efforts of the government being supplemented by the patriotic knitting needles of the Southern ladies. For some

The Southern women took up weaving, sewing and knitting in a desperate effort to clothe the soldiers. (Reproduced from the Volck etchings in the William R. Perkins Library of Duke University, Durham, North Carolina)

reason socks were their *forte* and one poor soldier complained that he had dozens of socks and but one shirt. Later on he would be lucky to have either.

The really serious deficiency in the Confederate army at this stage of the war was in weapons. The South had very little manufacturing capacity and, though great efforts were made to remedy this situation, Southern soldiers nearly always went into battle with inferior weapons. Smoothbore muskets and flintlocks were no match for the rifled muskets being turned out in their thousands from the Federal armoury at Springfield. Massed rifle fire was the great innovation of the American Civil War. Where a smoothbore was only

Lee's Colt pocket revolver in its velvet-lined case. On the back of the handgrip is engraved 'R.E.Lee Col. U.S.A.' suggesting that it was given to him before 1861, possibly on his retirement from West Point. (U.S. National Park Service)

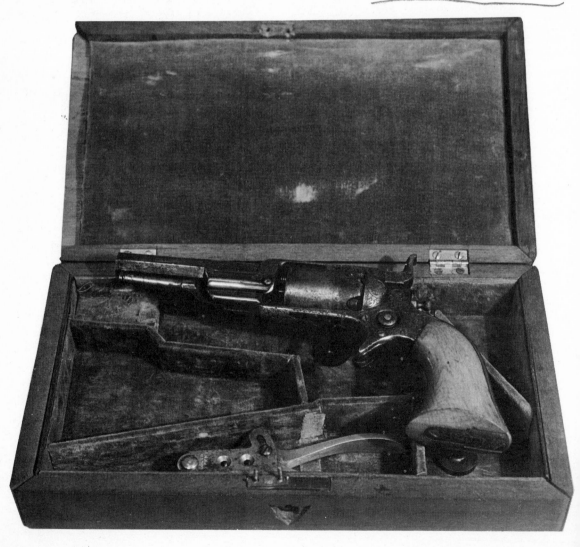

accurate up to about a hundred yards the rifle in skilful hands could be deadly up to five or six times that distance. This brutal fact was to make an enormous difference to tactics. No longer could infantrymen advance across open country and then run the last hundred yards to finish off the charge with the bayonet. This tactical lesson was to be cruelly learned by the dashing Southern infantry who battered themselves to pieces against prepared Federal positions under a deadly hail of rifle fire.

Just at the moment there was little Lee could do about this disparity in weapons, both hand-guns and artillery. Later, blockade-runners were to bring in large numbers of English and Belgian rifles and, more importantly, Federal defeats were to leave battlegrounds strewn with rifles, artillery, ammunition and an enormous range of luxurious stores. But Lee had to protect Richmond now and with the men and equipment that he found to his hand. As he assessed the strategic situation it was clear to him that his army was doomed if he continued Johnston's policy of allowing Mc-Clellan to take the initiative. McClellan would simply inch forward until his heavy siege guns could pound Richmond into submission. The only thing to do was to attack and force the Federals to fight under conditions where their superior numbers would not be able to tell. As he observed the great half circle of the Federal army in front of Richmond Lee prepared a plan, as imaginative as it was hopelessly unrealistic to execute with the inexperienced commanders and men at his disposal.

The first signs of activity on the part of their new commander did little to arouse enthusiasm amongst either his troops or the beleagured population of Richmond to their rear. Lee ordered his engineer officers to supervise the digging of a line of entrenchments between the enemy's lines and Richmond. The men were horrified. Digging in Virginia was something done by Negroes or Irishmen. Southern soldiers had enlisted to fight, not dig. In coming years they were to become some of the fastest diggers in history, once they had absorbed lessons about the firepower of the rifle and the new artillery which would have to be relearned by Englishmen and Frenchmen in the First World War. But the immediate reaction was summed up by Mary Boykin Chesnut: 'They are all once more digging for dear life. . . . Our chiefs continue to dampen and destroy the enthusiasm of all who go near

75

Digging was traditionally relegated to slaves and Lee's orders to the army to dig met with resentment. ABOVE Negro diggers at Savannah (Radio Times Hulton Picture Library)

them. So much entrenching and falling back destroys the *morale* of any army.' Lee now became known as the 'King of Spades' or 'Old Spade Lee. He keeps them digging so.'

Lee was rightly irritated at this archaic reaction to such sensible orders. 'Our people are opposed to work', he wrote to Jefferson Davis. In his opinion, 'There is nothing so military as labour, and nothing so important to any army as to save the lives of its soldiers' – an opinion shared by the soldiers once they had finished making their gentlemanly noises. In fact Lee's entrenchments were not so much a defensive measure as an integral part of his plan to take the war to the enemy. The idea was to hold the bulk of McClellan's army with just two entrenched divisions while the whole of the rest of the Confederate army attacked the Federal flank in overwhelming strength, rolling up the Federal line and threatening their line of communication with the base at the White House. It was a bold plan and depended on one risky assumption. McClellan must never realise how few men lay

76

between him and Richmond. But here Lee knew his man. McClellan was the most cautious of generals and throughout the campaign was totally convinced that he was heavily outnumbered by Lee.

Which flank should Lee attack? The Federal line lay in a fourteen-mile crescent between White Oak Swamp and Mechanicsville. As far as Lee could ascertain McClellan's left presented few opportunities for attack but his right, hopefully waiting for Washington and Jackson to release McDowell, seemed to be poorly protected. To find out if this was the case Lee sent his cavalry on one of the most dramatic reconnaissance expeditions of the war.

Jeb Stuart, the commander of the Confederate cavalry, was perhaps the most glamorous soldier of the Civil War. The cavalier of legend, magnificently dressed in gold braid, yellow sash and black ostrich plume, he found war an enormously entertaining game entirely suited to his own animal health

The dashing General Jeb Stuart at the head of his cavalry. (Radio Times Hulton Picture Library)

77

'The Burial of Latane', a lieutenant killed during
Stuart's ride around McClellan, shows that only
women, children and slaves were left on the plantations.
An engraving from a painting by W.D.Washington.
(The Museum of the Confederacy)

and strength. Naturally he had attracted to him much of the best blood of the South and the Confederate cavalry was for nearly the whole war to overshadow their opponents, who were once described as 'only a few scarecrow-men, who would dissolve partnership with their steeds at the first serious combined movement'. The stories about Jeb Stuart are legion – the balls he held in enemy territory, his personal banjo-player, his success with the ladies – but none compare with his great ride round McClellan's army with his 1,200 troopers. Much of it was pure braggadocio, such as when his troopers stopped to drink champagne from the general officers' stores, but as a reconnaissance expedition it was a complete success. McClellan's right flank was totally unprotected and so was his great depot at the White House.

Armed with this information Lee was ready to put his plan into action. There was only one thing more he wanted – the troops of Stonewall Jackson who were still busy defeating a quartet of Federal generals in the Shenandoah Valley, a hundred miles away from Richmond as the crow flies. Shortly before Stuart's ride, Jackson had fought and won two battles on consecutive days and Lee now thought that his Federal opponents had become so demoralised that it would be safe to bring virtually the whole of his command over to assist in the attack on McClellan. Orders were given to Jackson to slip away from the Valley using his cavalry to screen his departure from the enemy.

Riding ahead of his men, Jackson arrived on 23 June at Lee's headquarters for an eve-of-battle meeting with his fellow divisional commanders. Lee's great lieutenant was in striking contrast to his immaculate, if simply dressed, chief. In his weather-stained dingy uniform and old slouch hat the gaunt hero of the Valley Campaign looked tired and dishevelled. Seeing him after nearly two months of almost continuous riding and fighting, an observer remarked that 'horse and rider appeared worn down to the lowest point of flesh consistent with effective service'. But no one was worried by his condition. Spiritually and physically Jackson had the reputation of being a man of iron, gentle with his men but harsh in battle, a revengeful instrument of the Lord who apologised to his wife when he broke one of his own rules of conduct and fought a battle on a Sunday during the Valley Campaign. Of the three divisional commanders with whom he was to co-operate in the attack on McClellan Jackson

79

knew Harvey Hill best, his brother-in-law and like him a devout Presbyterian. The other two were another Hill, A.P.(Powell), the youngest of the four who was to be a great favourite of Lee, and finally the burly Longstreet, efficient and trustworthy but always seeking to dominate his own commander.

When the four men were assembled Lee quickly outlined his plan. Generals Huger and Magruder were to hold the trenches in front of Richmond with some 25,000 of the Confederate total of 80-85,000 men. Jackson was to maintain secrecy and bring his force up to outflank the Federal right. Immediately he received word that Jackson was in position Powell Hill was to push in the Federal outposts and attack their position at Beaver Dam Creek. It was not expected that there would be much resistance once Porter, Commander of the Federal right, realised he was outflanked. Then all four divisions were to push forward to threaten the Federal communications, at which point it was expected that McClellan would be forced to pull his men out of the trenches and fight a major battle to protect his base. There remained only the question of how long it would take Jackson to bring his troops up into positions. After some discussion 26 June, three days ahead, was decided on.

The success of Lee's first great battle, always described as the Seven Days although it in fact only lasted six (26 June-1 July 1862), was marred by a number of factors. The main problem was that it was a very complicated plan requiring co-ordination and strict adherence to schedule in very difficult country. Altogether it required the co-operation of six generals (including the two left in the trenches), none of whom had ever fought together before, under the overall control of a man who had never fought a battle and had virtually no staff. The countryside in which they were to fight, although well-known to Lee, was poorly mapped and was described by an artillery officer as 'for the most part covered by heavy pine forests and cypress swamps, and these traversed by many wood roads, or paths rather undistinguishable the one from the other'.

It was into one particular part of this confusing region that Jackson, who did not know the area, was expected to appear secretly out of the blue just at the time that Powell Hill advanced. It is hardly surprising that things went wrong. A deserter from Jackson's force gave the secret of his presence

80

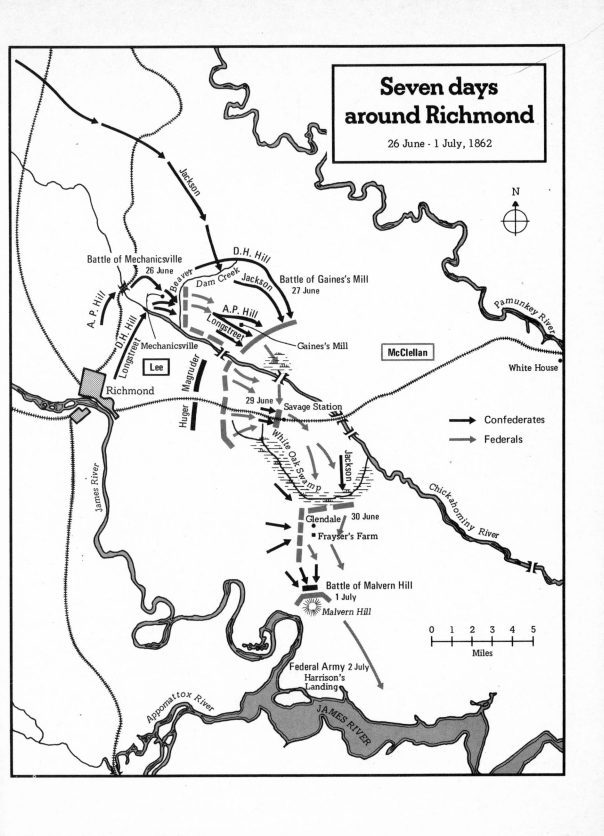

Seven days around Richmond

26 June - 1 July, 1862

Jackson

Battle of Mechanicsville
26 June

D.H. Hill

Beaver

Dam Creek

Jackson

Battle of Gaines's Mill
27 June

A. P. Hill

A.P. Hill

Longstreet

Gaines's Mill

D.H. Hill

Longstreet

Mechanicsville

Lee

Magruder

Richmond

Huger

McClellan

White House

Pamunkey River

29 June

Savage Station

White Oak Swamp

Jackson

Chickahominy River

James River

Glendale   30 June

Frayser's Farm

Battle of Malvern Hill
1 July

Malvern Hill

→ Confederates

→ Federals

0 1 2 3 4 5
Miles

Federal Army 2 July
Harrison's
Landing

Appomattox River

JAMES RIVER

N

away to McClellan. More seriously, Jackson underestimated the time he would require to get to his position on Powell Hill's left. Hill, eager for glory, got more and more impatient until eventually at three in the afternoon he crossed the river and moved forward. Pushing in the Federal outposts with ease he soon arrived at the very strong position which the Federals were defending at Beaver Dam Creek. To approach it his men had to cross a flat, open field which dipped down into the boggy bottom of the creek. On the other side of the creek, whose bridges had been destroyed, the bank rose steeply to where Federal infantry and artillery were well sited behind timber palisades. Unsupported by Jackson, who did not appear the whole day, and by Longstreet, whose men were unable to cross the Chickahominy until much later due to the absence of engineers to mend a bridge, Powell Hill's men were not able to make much impression on the Federal position. Southern courage there was in plenty, but as night fell the shattered survivors of his division were tied down by Federal fire power. Next morning Jackson's men were in position and, as Lee had expected, once the Federals found they were flanked they pulled out. What should have been a fairly bloodless operation cost over a thousand Confederate casualties because of Jackson's lateness and Powell Hill's impetuosity.

Very much the same thing happened on the next day. The Federal right retreated from its strong position on Beaver Dam Creek to an equally strong position on another creek behind Gaines Mill. Here again flat, open fields dipped to the swampy bottom of the creek with a steep hill on the other side. Once again Powell Hill, with Longstreet supporting him on his right, was the leading division. Once again Jackson, now with Harvey Hill in support, was supposed to flank the Federal right. But once again, poor maps, lack of knowledge of the country and confused communication with Lee ensured that Jackson arrived very late. Hill's battered men faced another day of forlorn bravery as they tried to storm the Federal position. But for one division it was hopeless. Then very late in the day order began to appear out of the confusion. Lee brought in Longstreet's division on the right to extend the line and one by one the brigades of Jackson and Harvey Hill began to appear on the left. At last between six and seven in the evening the whole Confederate line began to advance. As the light faded the tired Federals heard the blood-curdling rebel yell and at last they broke in the centre where the 4th Texas Regiment under Hood were the first to burst through the terrible Federal fire and break the line. Almost simultaneously the Federal left and right also broke and as darkness fell General Lee had won his first battle. As Lee wrote to Davis that night 'finally, after a severe contest of five hours' the enemy was entirely repulsed from the field. 'I grieve to state our loss in officers and men is great. We sleep on the field, and shall renew the contest in the morning.'

Lee's main task the following day was to ascertain McClellan's reaction to the defeat of his right wing. Lee expected the Federal general to pull his main force out of the trenches to fight him in one big battle on the north side of the river. But daybreak revealed that the Federals had all crossed over to the south, Richmond side, of the river. Where had they gone? There still existed the obvious danger that McClellan might attack the Richmond trenches in force. Magruder, in command of one section of the trenches, was in a state of near panic all day. His anxiety plus his habitual good living brought on an attack of severe indigestion which was treated with morphine, a factor which was to effect his performance for the remainder of the campaign. But in fact there was no sign of a threat on the Richmond front and it was clear that the men who had taken such a mauling at Gaines Mill had been withdrawn. Which way had they gone?

Slowly the answers came in. The cavalry discovered that the railway bridge across the Chickahominy had been destroyed, which made it clear that McClellan had cut himself off from his former supply depot at the White House and was not going to fight to protect it. Later in the day Stuart's cavalry confirmed this when they rode to the White House. With Stuart was Lee's son Rooney, Colonel of the 9th Virginia, who discovered on arrival that his own house was a burnt-out shell. Surrounding it were acres of half-burned Federal stores. The information provided by the cavalry left two possible alternative destinations for McClellan's retreat. Either he had gone back where he had started from – Fortress Monroe – or he had slipped across the back of the Richmond lines towards the James River. McClellan had got twenty-four hours lead on Lee before he discovered that it was to the James that the enemy were heading.

Foiled of his big battle on the north side of the river, Lee had to think out a completely new plan to try to destroy McClellan's army on the south side as it retreated. For the moment the initiative had shifted to the enemy and the Federals were able to move fast by abandoning much of their relatively useless equipment. On the morning of the fourth day Lee received news that the Federal trenches in front of Richmond had been abandoned without the Confederate pickets discovering what was happening. It was time to move and to move fast.

Lee's new plan was ready, but it was a plan that was going to require even more co-operation than had his original plan. And co-operation seemed to be the one talent of which the Confederate generals were conspicuously devoid. McClellan's expected route led almost due south across White Oak Swamp to the James River at Harrison's Landing. Traversing this route were four roads leading east and south-east out of Richmond like the spokes of a wheel. Lee's plan was for Jackson and Harvey Hill to follow McClellan's line of retreat and catch him in the rear, while the other four divisions of the army together with troops stationed south of the James under General Holmes should cut him off by marching along the roads out of Richmond. If all went well McClellan's army should be caught in a trap at Glendale, a point on McClellan's line of retreat easily accessible from all three of the Richmond roads which bore south-east. On the fourth road, the Williamsburg road which went due east, Magruder was to march to attack the Federal rear in conjunction with Jackson. The plan, though ingenious, was far too ambitious and what in fact happened was that McClellan was able to fight two fairly successful rearguard actions, both of which could have been overwhelming Confederate victories if everyone had turned up at the right place and at the right time.

The first action was on Sunday 29 June at a place called Savage's Station. It was here that Magruder was supposed to attack the rearguard in conjunction with Jackson. In fact the rearguard was far stronger than Lee had anticipated and Magruder, who had advanced very slowly, was reluctant to attack. What made him even more reluctant was the fact that Jackson, for the third time in four days, failed to show up for the battle. Jackson in fact spent the whole day mending the bridges across the Chickahominy, which had been destroyed as McClellan retreated, and did not start to cross the river till nightfall. At last, late in the afternoon, Magruder attacked the

84

The battle of Savage's
Station. (The Bettmann
Archive)

enemy by himself, but with his one division was unable to do
more than fight a hard fight so that during the night the
Federal rearguard were able to retreat to fight another battle
on the following day.

On the next day the same sort of misunderstanding and
mismanagement occurred. This was to be the great battle at
the Glendale cross-roads where three Confederate forces
were to converge and attack McClellan from in front and from
the flank while Jackson and Harvey Hill were to attack him
from the rear. In the end only two of the five divisions got into
action. The spearhead of the attack was supposed to come
from Huger, a contemporary of Lee but slow and rather
pompous. When he made contact with the enemy he stopped
his advance and did not attack. This puzzled Longstreet and
Powell Hill who were waiting for the signal of his attack to

commence their own. Eventually at five o'clock Lee ordered them to attack and they fought a savage but indecisive battle against the Federal rearguard. Huger, though close to the battle, failed to come in to their support. But once again the main question was where was Jackson? He and his brother-in-law Harvey Hill were supposed to push through White Oak Swamp and attack the Federal rear. Held up by Federal artillery, Jackson showed amazing lethargy and lack of initiative and for the second day running failed to show up for the battle. So once again McClellan's hard-fighting rearguard, in fact about half his army, were able to retreat in the night.

Now McClellan's army was nearly safe. The position which he had chosen for his final stand was virtually impregnable. Malvern Hill stands proud about a mile from the James River. Its western approaches could be covered by gunboats in the river. To the north of the hill, facing Lee's advance, was open ground and beyond lay broken and thickly-wooded country, covered with swamps which were only passable in a few places. The whole of this region was within range of the Federal batteries on the heights.

Everyone who saw Lee during the Seven Days remarked on the calmness and self-control with which he faced the disappointments brought on by the repeated failure of his divisional commanders to carry out his plans. It is some evidence of his frustration that he should have attempted to storm Malvern Hill with troops tired out after five days marching and fighting. When he argued that McClellan's troops must be demoralised and exhausted he was just fooling himself. The two battles fought by the Federal rearguard were clear evidence that they were not demoralised, and simple arithmetic could show that the Confederates had fought more and marched harder than their opponents. To attack Malvern Hill was suicidal. In a series of unco-ordinated movements division after division tried to storm the hill, only to fall back with terrible losses. As night fell both sides had had enough. The Seven Days were over. During the night McClellan withdrew his men to the riverside under cover of his gunboats and Lee, after a half-hearted attempt to bring the Federals once more to battle, withdrew his men to Richmond.

Lee had much to think about. His first great battle or series of battles was the whole of his apprenticeship as a commander in the field. It was a tough education. Gone was any idea that the Federal soldiers were Northern weaklings who would run at the first sight of Southern courage. Badly generalled as they were, the Federals had fought all the way from Mechanicsville to Malvern Hill and the grim list of Confederate casualties proved it. There were just not enough men in the Confederacy to provide for this kind of victory. Richmond was saved, but McClellan's troops had lived to fight another day. Whose fault was it? One of Lee's best characteristics was his willingness to take responsibility and in his report on the campaign he made no scapegoats. It is noticeable, however, that Magruder and Huger disappeared from his immediate command. Of the two, Huger had proved a complete disaster when he failed to attack in support of Longstreet at

Edwin Francis Jennison, killed at Malvern Hill, 1862. (Brady Collection, Library of Congress)

Glendale. Magruder had done well in the past and, in particular, had made a good job of persuading McClellan that there were far more men in the Richmond trenches than in fact there were. But he was irresolute in attack and needed too much support for the independent role that Lee envisioned for his divisional commanders.

The real failure in the Seven Days Campaign, however, was Jackson. Lee himself never criticised him, but from that day to the present everyone else has wondered what happened to the hero of the Valley in his first campaign under Lee's command. The series of excuses to explain Jackson's failure to appear or exert himself on every single action are hardly convincing in their totality. Good generals have one or two bad days but not so many in a row. Some people have said that he wanted to protect his troops who had done so much fighting in the Valley; others that he resented serving under another man. Neither reason seems much like the Jackson of either the past or the future. Almost certainly the reason for his failure was stress – stress brought on by exhaustion from his two months' constant activity and responsibility in the Valley and the task of getting his troops across Virginia to fight in front of Richmond. What he needed was a few nights' good sleep. Lee never had any doubts as to his real competence and was soon to send him north in an independent role. Lee was right. Jackson and Lee were to become firm friends and great admirers of each other's talents in the ten months of audacious teamwork that was to astonish the world and frustrate the Federal generals before Jackson's untimely death.

Lee himself, despite the only partial success of his campaign, was now a hero. Richmond was saved, and Richmond and the whole of the South were grateful. The daring and aggression of his strategy were much admired by people who had watched with anguish as Johnston's army had slowly moved backwards towards the Confederate capital. 'Granny' Lee and the 'King of Spades' were forgotten, to be replaced in the course of a week's hard fighting by the image of a noble, grey-haired cavalier in whom civilian and soldier alike had total confidence and a fixed and unshakeable faith in all he did. With such a general and such an army the South must win and the rightness of her cause would thus be broadcast to the world. Such faith was a responsibility for any man, but General Lee and the Army of Northern Virginia did much to sustain it in the course of the following year.

OPPOSITE Thomas Jonathan Jackson by J.A.Elder. Jackson was the most able of Lee's generals and gained his nickname 'Stonewall' Jackson from a promise to stand as firm as a stone wall at the first battle of Bull Run. (In the collection of the Corcoran Gallery of Art; Gift of W.W.Corcoran)

4
Maryland, My Maryland

THE ARMY OF NORTHERN VIRGINIA had won its first great battle and a legend had been born. Already what Winston Churchill called the 'deathless' army was taking its future shape. The volunteers, who had arrived in Richmond the year before with every conceivable piece of equipment which they could ransack from their homes, had now taken on that lean, hungry, sun-burned, unshaven appearance which was the hallmark of the Confederate soldier. It was not yet the scarecrow army of the end of the war, but already much of the surplus gear had been discarded. Federal rifles at Gaines Mill had taught the grey-clad infantrymen that the day of the revolver and the bowie knife as weapons of war was over and they were discarded as so much extra weight. This was a rifle war and Billie Yank, Mr Lincoln's boy in blue, had obligingly left plenty of rifles in the swamps and pine forests of the Peninsula. It was also a marching war and the passage of the army was to be marked by a stream of litter, as all that seemed too heavy or too hot to carry around in the Virginian summer was thrown by the wayside. Greatcoats, spare blankets, heavy boots and tents were all discarded as the private soldier reduced his equipment to a portable minimum. A veteran has detailed this minimum for us:

One man, one slouch hat, one jacket, one shirt, one pair of pants, one pair of drawers, one pair of shoes, and one pair of socks. His baggage was one blanket, one rubber blanket, and one haversack. The haversack generally contained smokers tobacco and a pipe, and a small piece of soap, with temporary additions of apples, persimmons, blackberries, and such other commodities as he could pick up on the march.

The piece of soap was small indeed, and unfriendly critics said you could smell the army long before you saw them. But it was an army of great humour and great confidence in itself who felt that any material deficiencies could quickly be made up 'at the expense of Mr Lincoln.

Just at the moment, however, the army was not marching and was nowhere near northern Virginia. As Lee and Davis discussed the military situation after the battle of the Seven Days they had much to worry about. The position in Virginia was very similar to what it had been when McClellan first landed on the Peninsula. The movement of Jackson to Richmond had allowed the junction of the several armies he had defeated in his Valley Campaign. This force was now

PREVIOUS PAGES Federal troops searching for arms in a house in southern Maryland. (British Museum)

A Confederate soldier with his minimum of equipment. (The Bettmann Archive)

93

after 7 DAYS
situation BAD

V.o

under the command of the confident General John Pope, who boasted that his headquarters would be on his horse and that he would make no provision for retreat. At the moment this braggart, who had won some success in the west, was moving south to threaten Richmond's railway communications with the rest of the Confederacy. Meanwhile McClellan remained at Harrison's Landing, only some twenty miles from Richmond, and a third Federal general, Burnside, was at the foot of the peninsula with troops on ships ready to reinforce either Pope or McClellan. Information from spies and scouts led Lee to suppose, fairly accurately, that altogether the Federals had at least double his numbers in Virginia.

There was little likelihood of Lee being reinforced from the other theatres of the war. For the situation in the western Confederacy was even worse than in Virginia. Here lay the great wealth of the cotton states, the iron deposits of Tennessee, great ports and cities such as New Orleans, Memphis, Nashville and St Louis. But in this enormous sweep of territory from the Appalachians to Texas, a front of over a thousand miles, the feeble resources of the rebels were stretched to breaking point as they tried to garrison every important place and keep large armies in the field. The west was always to be more vulnerable than the east. It is a strange aspect of the American Civil War that for four years the eyes of the world were to be fixed on the fortunes of two great armies manoeuvring in Virginia, protecting their respective capitals and fighting great battles, while the war was quietly won for the North in the west. The advantages for the Federals in this theatre were enormous. Nature had provided them with superb communications for invasion. The Mississippi-Missouri-Ohio river system threatened the South at a hundred points. Except for the two great tributaries of the Ohio, the Tennessee and the Cumberland, the currents of the rivers ran for the invader. All the great steamboat manufacturing centres were in the North as were most of the great river men. Armed steamboats and gunboats meant that thousands of men could be moved with little danger or fatigue from point to point at a speed that made marching men seem like snails. And the rivers, unlike the railways, were not vulnerable to the raids of the Confederate cavalry. It is hardly too much to say that in this, supposedly the first great railway war in history, it was the Mississippi steamboat which ensured victory for the North.

Jefferson Thompson's guerrillas shooting at Federal boats on the Mississippi. (Radio Times Hulton Picture Library)

The New Orleans docks in
1862 showing the
accumulated cotton due to
the blockade. (Radio Times
Hulton Picture Library)

The first six months of 1862 had seen a whole series of
Confederate disasters in the west. In February an amphibious
force under the command of the up-and-coming general
U.S. Grant had captured two key forts on the Tennessee and
Cumberland rivers, thus making the whole of northern
Tennessee with its resources in men and minerals virtually
untenable to the Confederates. The way seemed open for an
invasion of the central Confederacy and the destruction of
the main east-west artery, the railway which ran from
Charleston to Memphis via the two key junctions of Atlanta,
Georgia and Chattanooga, Tennessee. But, as in the east, the
Federal generals consistently overestimated the strength of

the Confederates in this region and it was not to be until 1863 that Chattanooga fell and the way was open for Sherman's famous invasion of Georgia. Before then, however, some of the bloodiest battles of the war were to be fought in this key area of Tennessee. Farther west the Confederate position looked equally doomed. Northern naval and river power seized New Orleans in April and Memphis in June. Only Confederate control of Vicksburg prevented the Federal occupation of the entire Mississippi Valley and the complete severance of Texas, Louisiana and Arkansas from the rest of the South.

Although Lee was not made commander-in-chief until the very end of the war, he was always very aware of the need to bring about some co-ordination between Confederate activity in the Virginian and western theatres of the war. In his view there was only one way for the enormous frontiers of the Confederacy to be defended. With such limited resources it was hopeless to sit back and attempt to check Federal invasion. The truth of this had been quite clearly seen in the contest between Johnston and McClellan. Once a patient general like McClellan, with enormous superiority in numbers, was able to bring up his siege guns the defence of such a city as Richmond would be hopeless. No, the only answer was to seize the initiative and attack. If the Confederate armies advanced and won battles in the field then and only then would the Confederacy win its independence. And to get the best possible results it would be necessary to advance simultaneously in both the east and the west to prevent the Federals from reinforcing either sector. Lee always had this end in mind – two great battles, one in Kentucky and the other in Maryland, could win the war.

Deliberately to seek battle was obviously a risky policy for generals who were almost certain to be outnumbered. But Lee had confidence in his own skill. Once he could take the initiative he felt sure that he could make the most of his smaller numbers by concentrating his forces on the enemy where he was least expecting it. This was the basis of all his successful actions. Where he was forced to slog it out face to face with the enemy he often did well, as at Gaines Mill, because of the superb fighting qualities of his soldiers; but it was an expensive policy whose eventual result must be disaster for the Confederacy. The brutal arithmetic of a nation with only a quarter of the manpower of its opponent

97

was only too obvious. But subtle and imaginative attack could bring him victory in battle and eventually, it was hoped, victory in the war.

Victory in battle could have many results beyond the mere destruction of the enemy's resources. A run of Confederate victories could so weaken public opinion in the North that the attempt to bring the South to heel would be abandoned. There was plenty of evidence of dissatisfaction with the war, now that it was obvious that it was not to be the short and easy victory which had attracted the first flush of volunteers. Perhaps even more important in Southern minds was the effect of Southern victories on European opinion, particularly that of England and of France. Before secession it had been an article of faith that England would recognise Southern independence and would use her naval power to curb the North. Much of this optimism was based on the economic interdependence between the South and England. Cotton manufacture was England's main industry and it was felt that Northern interference with her supplies of raw materials would never be tolerated. Such economic arguments were backed up by a firm belief that the English ruling classes would sympathise with the aristocratic society of the South, recognising them for the gentlemen they were, engaged in a struggle against the forces of Mammon and egalitarianism.

There was some substance in these Southern hopes. Many Englishmen did support the Confederacy, for the reasons above and also because they saw the Southern challenge as another example of that desire for self-determination which they were always prepared to support in other countries, if not in Ireland. Many admired the gallantry and courage of the South as they fought such an unequal contest. But by 1862 a substantial body of opinion overseas saw the ultimate hopelessness of the Southern cause and the overriding attitude was to keep clear of the whole business. And indeed, although the English aristocracy might approve of Southern institutions, this was hardly true of most of the middle and proletarian classes in England who were still waiting for a clear lead on what seemed to them the real moral issue in question. What was Lincoln going to do about slavery?

As the war became more and more of an all-consuming issue Lincoln's attitude was changing. In his Inaugural Address and in the early months of the war he was quite clear in his aims. He would fight to save the Union but also to protect the

98

A *Punch* cartoon of April 1862 on the slavery issue. (Radio Times Hulton Picture Library)

OBERON AND TITANIA.

Oberon (Mr. President Lincoln). "I DO BUT BEG A LITTLE **NIGGER** BOY, TO BE MY HENCHMAN."

Titania (Miss Virginia). "SET YOUR HEART AT REST, THE **NORTHERN** LAND BUYS NOT THE CHILD OF ME."

existing institutions of the country, including slavery. His views on slavery were indeed very similar to those of Lee. He did not feel that the two races could live in freedom, side by side, and approved of gradual emancipation and subsidised colonisation. But he was under enormous pressure to take more positive action from the more radical members of the Republican party. As the months went by and Lincoln began to show his real strength, he was himself feeling his way to a far more radical position. The war had gone too far for a simple return to the ante-bellum situation. It seemed

99

inconceivable that, following a Northern victory, slavery could continue to be the foundation of the beaten rebels' society. Lincoln tried many compromises before he adopted an all-out revolutionary approach to this problem. He tried to convert the border states who had been loyal to the Union by offering them a system of compensated emancipation. But despite much support for Lincoln's scheme the representatives of these states remained loyal to slavery. All the time that Lincoln was experimenting along these lines Northern newspapers and the more radical members of his Cabinet were urging him to adopt a far more aggressive attitude both towards the South and slavery. Southerners were in armed rebellion against their government and, as rebels, they must be stripped of everything they had. Recaptured Southern territory could be wasted; Southern property could be seized. And slavery, the root of Southern wealth and the bane of the nation, must be abolished by proclamation, using the war powers of the President.

Certainly to make such a proclamation could well be a valuable weapon of war. It would be an obvious encouragement to slaves to run away, thus helping to ruin Southern agriculture, and it might ultimately have the effect of providing the North with regiments of Negro soldiers only too glad to make war on their former masters. But Lincoln, like most white Americans, was horrified at the thought of race war and slave rebellion. Even more to the point he was worried about the reactions of white citizens and white soldiers to such a radical step. Men had rushed forward to fight for the Union but they would be unlikely to be so keen to fight for the Negro. Two Northern states were so race-conscious that they had passed laws prohibiting free Negro immigration. Immigrants in the east had rioted when they were faced with Negro competition in the labour market. Anti-Negro feeling was strong everywhere and perhaps particularly in the army.

The growing split in Washington as to the aims of the war and the methods by which it should be fought were paralleled in the Federal army. McClellan, now discredited as a general by his failure before Richmond, stood for limited war and limited aims. A Democrat who would stand for President against Lincoln in 1864, his objective was to restore the Union and no more. He believed that the best way to do this and provide for a healthy post-war world was to confine the war to building up overwhelming military strength to defeat the Confederate army and to do as little as possible to alienate Southern civilian opinion by vindictive policies. The man who had just been appointed to take command in northern Virginia, Pope, was exactly the opposite. On taking command, he had issued a series of savage orders which showed clearly the degree to which radical Northern opinion was prepared to go in its intention of punishing as well as defeating rebels. Supplies in rebel territory could be commandeered, to be paid for at the end of the war only if the owner could demonstrate his loyalty to the Union. Men who refused to take an oath of allegiance to the Union could be forced to leave home, to be shot as traitors if they ever fell into Federal hands again. Pope's orders were an invitation to his troops to loot, which was gratefully accepted, but some of the harsher of his orders were in fact never carried out. He was a bully and a braggart, but his bark was worse than his rather ineffective bite. Lee loathed him. Indeed he was the only one of the many Federal generals sent against him that he really felt bitterly opposed to. There is a sting in his correspondence when he discusses the immediate necessity of 'suppressing' the 'miscreant' Pope. But Lee also had a very low opinion of Pope as a general and, as it turned out, his judgment was sound.

Washington now had to decide what to do with McClellan's army and McClellan himself. Led by the Secretary of War, Stanton, there was much pressure on the President to dismiss his general-in-chief and abandon the whole strategy of trying to capture Richmond from the peninsula. In vain did McClellan demand more men or put forward a very sensible plan to cross the James and attack Richmond from the south and south-east. A military failure and a political threat, his reputation was at its lowest and his opinions ignored. The only problem was that he was very popular with his men and Washington dreaded the effect on morale of dismissing him. For the moment Lincoln was content to replace him as general-in-chief by the western general, Halleck, an equally cautious soldier, but leave him in command of his army huddled at Harrison's Landing on the peninsula.

Lee himself felt sure that McClellan would eventually be ordered to retire from the peninsula and made his plans accordingly. Jackson and Powell Hill were sent north to check the progress of Pope, while the rest of the army remained in the vicinity of Richmond to watch McClellan, ready to move to Jackson's assistance as soon as McClellan's soldiers started to move down the James. Lee had reorganised the army somewhat since the Seven Days. Aware that some of his command problems had arisen from the difficulty of dealing directly with six divisional commanders, he placed the divisions in two big corps or wings under Jackson and Longstreet, who had emerged as the other strong man in the army.

A sign that Lee's reading of the situation was correct was the reported departure of Burnside's men up Chesapeake Bay. Clearly he was going to reinforce Pope. It was obvious that McClellan would soon follow him. Without waiting for his former rival's actual embarcation, Lee ordered the bulk of Longstreet's corps out of the Richmond trenches and prepared to move forward to hit Pope before he could be reinforced by Burnside and McClellan. Once again Lee gambled on McClellan's inactivity as he stripped Richmond of her defenders, and once again he gambled quite correctly. McClellan started to move almost as soon as Longstreet, but he moved incredibly slowly. He hated Pope and all he stood for. Moreover, he was furious with Washington whom he thought had let him down very badly after his campaign against Lee's overwhelming numbers, and it seems quite likely that he actually wanted Pope to be defeated. At least that seems to have been in his mind when he wrote to his wife: 'I think the result of their machinations will be that Pope will be badly thrashed within ten days, and they will be glad to turn over the redemption of their affairs to me.'

Pope had now got himself into an extremely vulnerable position. His advance had been checked when his leading corps was defeated by Jackson at the battle of Cedar Mountain on 9 August. Now he had retreated and was in the triangle formed by the Rappahannock and its tributary, the Rapidan. At this stage, for the first and only time in the campaign, Lee outnumbered Pope. If he could only get men behind Pope to cut off his retreat across the Rappahannock, he could totally destroy the Federal army long before reinforcements arrived from Burnside or McClellan. However, inadequate co-operation between Lee's cavalry commanders spoiled this move and Pope was able to retreat with little loss behind the Rappahannock.

This was a far stronger position. The fords were well guarded and Pope was being reinforced almost daily by units from Burnside and McClellan. Things were beginning to look a little dangerous for Lee. It was time to act. Lee's plan demonstrated his characteristic boldness. The main idea was to draw Pope to the north and west, away from his reinforcements, and there force him into a disadvantageous battle and destroy him. It was almost a complete success and this campaign leading up to the second battle of Bull Run indicated that at last the various units of the Army of Northern Virginia were beginning to co-operate as a team.

Once again Lee took an enormous risk by dividing his army in the face of the enemy. On the night of 25 August Jackson's corps of 24,000 men began moving towards the upper reaches of the Rappahannock, leaving Longstreet with 28,000 men to face Pope's army which had now been brought up to some 80,000. Jackson was about to begin a quite phenomenal march and to ensure greater speed he ordered his men to leave their haversacks behind. No doubt his men, excited at the prospect of action, hoped soon to replace them at the expense of the Federal government. Jackson's route lay across the upper fords of the Rappahannock and then north behind the Bull Run Mountains. On the first day his 'foot cavalry' completed twenty-five miles. Poor though Pope's reconnaissance was, Jackson's move was noted, but not its significance. Not realising that Jackson was in command of nearly half Lee's whole army, Pope thought that he was just leading a raid into the Shenandoah Valley and continued to look at Longstreet across the river. The next day Jackson crossed the mountains through the gorge-like pass of Thoroughfare Gap and placed himself firmly across Pope's line of communications, some twenty-five miles north of the Rappahannock. Virtually unresisted, Jackson's troops entered into an orgy of destruction. It was nearly midnight when the Confederates, who had marched fifty-four miles in two days, captured Manassas Junction, Pope's main supply depot which was piled high with what seemed to the exhausted and half-starved soldiers an unbelievable store of plenty. Jackson put a guard on the whiskey and told his troops to take as much as they could carry. How they ever managed to fight after they had stuffed themselves full is one of the many unsolved mysteries of the war. The feast finished, Jackson set fire to the depot and thousands of dollars' worth of bacon, salt pork and flour disappeared in the flames.

Pope had little idea of what was going on but at last he

Jackson's troops pillaging
the Federal supply depot of
Manassas Junction.
(British Museum)

realised that Jackson was loose to his rear. It seemed a heaven-
sent opportunity to surround and destroy him. This was
exactly what Lee had hoped Pope's reaction would be.
Already he had sent Longstreet off on the same march as
Jackson, leaving only one division behind the Rappahannock.
Jackson himself completed the destruction of Manassas
Junction and then moved north-west to Groveton, about
twelve miles from Thoroughfare Gap, where he took up a
strong position and prepared for the arrival of Longstreet
through the pass.

The confused Pope arrived at Manassas only to find that
the bird had flown. Following up one of Jackson's many false
trails, he decided that his elusive enemy had gone to Centreville
and ordered his equally confused corps commanders to move
there. Late on 28 August Jackson, who had his men concealed

in woods on rising ground near Groveton some six miles from Centreville, decided to put Pope out of his agony. Aware that Longstreet should come out of the mountains the next morning, he deliberately exposed his troops as one of Pope's divisions came marching across his front on their way to Centreville. A hard stand-up fight followed until nightfall. At last Pope felt he had Jackson in the bag. His orders were again countermanded and all divisions were directed to converge on Groveton. He still did not seem to realise what Lee and Longstreet were doing and made little attempt to defend Thoroughfare Gap to keep the two parts of Lee's army separated. Later that same day, while Jackson was attracting Pope's attention at Groveton, Longstreet's men fought their way with little difficulty through the pass. On the next morning as the whole of his command resumed their march down into the plain, the sound of cannon announced that Jackson was already engaged.

The country where the second battle of Bull Run was

Lee watching the fighting at Thoroughfare Gap during the second battle of Bull Run. (The Bettmann Archive)

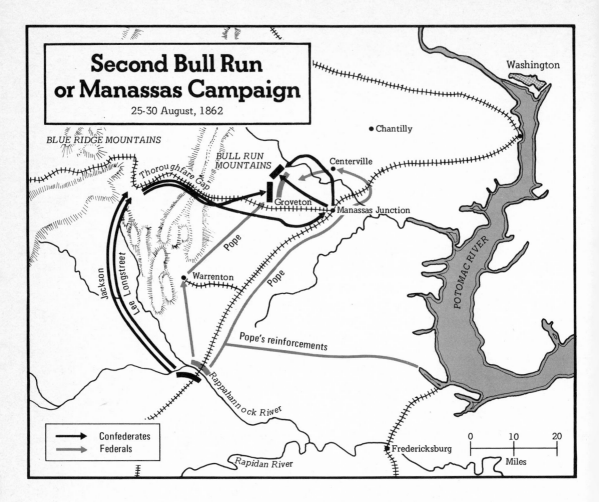

Second Bull Run or Manassas Campaign

25-30 August, 1862

BLUE RIDGE MOUNTAINS

BULL RUN MOUNTAINS

Thoroughfare Gap

Chantilly

Centerville

Groveton

Manassas Junction

Jackson

Lee Longstreet

Pope

Pope

Warrenton

Pope's reinforcements

Washington

POTOMAC RIVER

Rappahannock River

Rapidan River

Fredericksburg

→ Confederates
→ Federals

0   10   20

Miles

fought was strikingly different from the swampland of the
Seven Days. Largely free of obstruction, it was an area of
gently rolling ground, criss-crossed by a network of roads and
country lanes which made it easy to shift troops. Jackson's
entrenched position was quite strong. On his left he had the
stream of Bull Run while his right was open, ready for
Longstreet's men to take up their position as they came down
from the mountains. Both flanks were guarded by cavalry.
His tactics were simple – to stay there until he was reinforced.
Pope, with over three times Jackson's numbers, acted fairly
sensibly, except that he still did not seem to realise that
Longstreet was coming. The main body was to attack
Jackson frontally, whilst some 25,000 men under McDowell
and Porter were to press an attack on his right flank. If they
had done this Jackson might well have been destroyed. But

the flank attack was never made. The reasons are somewhat obscure, but after the battle, Porter, a McClellan man, was accused of deliberate obstruction if not downright treachery. What probably happened was that Porter thought that Longstreet's command had already come up on Jackson's right. This was what General Stuart who commanded the cavalry on that flank wanted him to think and he had ordered his men to raise the dust in order to fool the Federals. Meanwhile Pope launched attack after attack against Jackson in the afternoon of this second day of the battle, 29 August. Jackson was very hard-pressed, especially on his left where the red-shirted red-haired Powell Hill once again bore the brunt of a battle. An unfinished railway line lay in front of Jackson's position and by the evening of the second day it was cluttered with dead bodies, but Jackson finished the day in the same position as he had started it. While Jackson fought, Longstreet came up on his right completely unopposed.

The morning of the third day was very hot. The Confederate line, now complete, was shaped like a V with its apex away from the enemy. At the apex were massed artillery ready to fire along either Jackson's or Longstreet's front. Pope still ignored Longstreet and at midday he ordered a general assault against Jackson's right. The Confederates watched for two hours as the Federals got into position and began to move forward. The menacing tramp of feet and the rumble of the gun carriages came nearer and nearer. Then about two o'clock there was a moment of silence before the massed Confederate artillery roared into the Federal left and Jackson's men took up their fighting positions. But still the Federals came on. Two hours of fighting followed in which some of Jackson's men ran out of ammunition and had to content themselves with heaving rocks at their opponents. But all the time the Confederate artillery was firing into the Federal flank and at last, just before four o'clock, the Federal left broke. Longstreet and Lee had been waiting for this moment. Now was the time for the counter-attack by the unscathed soldiers of Longstreet's command. Soon the whole line was in motion, driving the enemy from the battlefield. It was not quite a rout and a vigorous rearguard action enabled Pope to get his beaten army across Bull Run and back to Centreville. Rain in the night and the exhaustion of the soldiers prevented the Confederates from pressing the pursuit.

Once again Lee's audacity had worked and won him a great

The Second Battle of Bull Run

ABOVE Edwin Forbes's sketch
of the battle with
instructions to the engraver.
It was common for the war
artists to make a rough
drawing of the battle
in progress and send it
back to their newspaper
to be redrawn and engraved

for publication. (Library
of Congress)
OPPOSITE ABOVE A photograph
of the same stone house which
appears in Forbes's sketch.
(Library of Congress)
RIGHT Pope's army fleeing
from the battle.
(Library of Congress)

victory, but once again his enemy had escaped complete destruction. Next morning Lee felt he had to press his advantage and hit the dejected Federals again while they were still demoralised. The footsore soldiers set off on a march to outflank Pope at Centreville. But now there was none of that energy and determination which had taken them to Manassas, and when they clashed with the Federals at Chantilly, to the west of Centreville, Lee realised that his men had had enough for the moment and that there was plenty of fight left in his enemy. He decided to rest his army before the next stage of his campaign. Meanwhile Pope retreated to Washington. In three months Lee had cleared Virginia of Union soldiers. It was time to be going somewhere else and the next place was called Maryland.

Lee had many good reasons for invading Maryland. Many of his best officers were Marylanders and they had assured him that the mere presence of a Confederate army would give place to a mass rising in his favour. This was an optimistic sentiment that was at the same moment being pronounced on the other side of the Appalachians where General Bragg was leading another army into Kentucky. But in fact there were risings in neither place. More certain was the purely administrative reason for invasion. Lee's army had eaten all that Virginia could produce; Maryland could feed him for a few months, the food to be paid for of course. Lee would not imitate Pope's methods of treating an invaded country. Finally the invasion would have an enormous effect on public opinion. It was one thing to have a rebel army in Virginia, quite another when that army marched into Maryland and began to threaten the great cities of the North. One great victory there and who knows what might happen. A scared Lincoln might listen at last to the peace party. England might recognise the Confederacy. Yes, there were good reasons for Lee to invade Maryland, risky though it was to take his army so far from home.

On 3 September the Confederate army moved off, crossed the Potomac thirty miles upstream from Washington and entered the Union, the bands playing 'Maryland, my Maryland' as they marched. Curious eyes followed their progress as they moved into the town of Frederick, but even the most optimistic Southern soldier could detect little enthusiasm. The people were in fact amazed that this bunch of derelicts had defeated great generals like McClellan and

OPPOSITE Lee's proclamation to the people of Maryland inviting them freely to choose their destiny. (Maryland Historical Society)

PROCLAMATION OF GENERAL LEE.

HEADQUARTERS ARMY N. VA. }
Near Fredericktown, Sept. 8, 1862. }

TO THE PEOPLE OF MARYLAND:

It is right that you should know the purpose that has brought the Army under my command within the limits of your State, so far as that purpose concerns yourselves.

The People of the Confederate States have long watched, with the deepest sympathy, the wrongs and outrages that have been inflicted upon the Citizens of a Commonwealth, allied to the States of the South by the strongest social, political and commercial ties. They have seen with profound indignation their sister States deprived of every right, and reduced to the condition of a conquered province.

Under the pretense of supporting the constitution, but in violation of its most valuable provisions, your Citizens have been arrested and imprisoned upon no charge, and contrary to all forms of law; the faithful and manly protest against this outrage made by the venerable and illustrious Marylander whom in better days no citizen appealed for right in vain, was treated with scorn and contempt; the government of your chief city has been usurped by armed strangers; your Legislature has been dissolved by the unlawful arrest of its members; freedom of the press and of speech has been suppressed; words have been declared offences by an arbitrary decree of the Federal Executive, and citizens ordered to be tried by a military commission for what they may dare to speak.

Believing that the people of Maryland possessed a spirit too lofty to submit to such a government, the people of the South have long wished to aid you in throwing off this foreign yoke to enable you again to enjoy the inalienable rights of freemen, and restore independence and sovereignty to your State. In obedience to this wish, our army has come among you, and is prepared to assist you with the power of its arms in regaining the rights of which you have been despoiled. This, Citizens of Maryland, is our mission, so far as you are concerned. No restraint upon your free will is intended, no intimidation will be allowed. Within the limits of this army, at least, Marylanders shall once more enjoy their ancient freedom of thought and speech. We know no enemies among you, and will protect all of every opinion. It is for you to decide your destiny, freely and without constraint. This Army will respect your choice, whatever it may be; and while the Southern people will rejoice to welcome you to your natural position among them, they will only welcome you when you come of your own free will.

R. E. LEE, General Commanding.

Pope. The forced marches and the fighting had played havoc with their already meagre clothing. Thousands of soldiers had no shoes, many barefoot stragglers never in fact reaching the Potomac; jackets were weather-stained and torn, trousers ragged and often in holes. But they had a certain air about them and did not seem to be quite the horde of bandits that they at first appeared. One thing which really struck the observers was their good discipline and the absence of any vandalism. 'These bundles of rags, these cough-racked, diseased and starved men', as one lady described them, caused less damage on their way through Maryland than the supposedly friendly Union army.

The Union army was at this moment licking its wounds in Washington. Pope's failure set Lincoln a real problem. Who could replace him? There was in fact only one man who had the confidence of the army and he was the one man who

Longstreet's corps crossing the Blue Ridge from the Shenandoah to the Rappahannock. (Radio Times Hulton Picture Library)

Washington wanted out – General McClellan, the exponent of limited war, whose delay in reinforcing Pope had deprived him of two vital divisions at Bull Run and whose colleague Porter had seemed to do his best to lose the battle. But with Lee loose in Maryland the army needed a commander quickly and finally Lincoln disregarded his advisers and reinstated the now somewhat tarnished Young Napoleon.

Lee was delighted. If there was one thing needed to make his Maryland campaign a success it was McClellan in command of the enemy. With complete aplomb he decided to divide his army in four parts in the middle of hostile territory. Lee's communications were threatened by the continued Federal occupation of the town of Harper's Ferry, at the junction of the Potomac and Shenandoah rivers. The town had to be captured before the army could safely proceed farther north. Jackson was ordered to recross the Potomac above Harper's Ferry and attack the town from the hills to the west. Two other units were sent by different routes to attack from the north and the east. Meanwhile Longstreet's corps was to cross South Mountain, a northern extension of the Blue Ridge, and advance towards Hagerstown near the Pennsylvania border. Lee expected Jackson to have little trouble capturing Harper's Ferry and arrangements were made for a general rendezvous of the whole army near Hagerstown. Longstreet, always cautious, remonstrated with Lee on the folly of dividing the army. But Lee saw little danger. By the time McClellan knew where he was Lee expected to be on the Susquehanna in southern Pennsylvania.

No doubt Lee was right, but for once luck was not on his side. As his troops marched out of Frederick on their various assignments, three cigars wrapped up in a piece of paper were left behind. When McClellan's army moved in this piece of paper was shown to the commanding general. It was a copy of Lee's orders showing where all the units had gone and above all demonstrating that the army was divided. For once in his life McClellan moved quite fast when he saw his chance – fast for him that is but not fast enough to destroy Lee. Within hours of seeing Lee's order McClellan's army were ready to continue their march. But they did not actually set out till the morning of the next day, 13 September. When they reached South Mountain they found the two passes of Turner's Gap and Crampton's Gap strongly guarded by Harvey Hill's rearguard. In the end this gallant defence would of course be overwhelmed by McClellan's superior numbers. But every hour counted as Longstreet brought his corps back from the north and Jackson completed his preparations for the capture of Harper's Ferry. By the night of 14 September Hill had done enough. Twenty-four hours had been gained for Lee and all he had to do now was to withdraw Hill and reassemble the whole of his army at Harper's Ferry.

This is what anyone but Lee would have done and it was what Longstreet advised. But Lee was not Longstreet. That night he received a message from Jackson that Harper's Ferry would fall on the following morning. Lee decided that he would stand and fight McClellan. The place where he decided to make his stand was called Sharpsburg, a small town just behind a tributary of the Potomac called the Antietam Creek and some twelve miles from Harper's Ferry. Lee's decision was to bring about the bloodiest single day of the whole war.

On the morning of 15 September the 18,000 men commanded by Longstreet and D.H.Hill were in their positions behind the Antietam Creek, a country of farmland with occasional woods. About three hours' march away McClellan had some 90,000 Federal soldiers. And yet incredibly he did not attack on either 15 or 16 September. In forty-eight hours the situation had changed a bit. Harper's Ferry fell, as Jackson

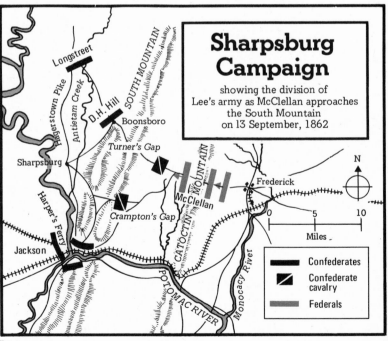

Sharpsburg Campaign

showing the division of
Lee's army as McClellan approaches
the South Mountain
on 13 September, 1862

had promised, on the morning of the 15th. Twenty-four hours later Jackson rode up at the head of the first contingents of his corps, now released to come to the assistance of Lee. By the beginning of the 17th, when McClellan actually decided to attack, Lee had 28,000 men at Sharpsburg and 15,000 more either on the way or at Harper's Ferry. Even so he was still outnumbered by more than three to one at the start of the battle. McClellan thought he had 100,000 men!

McClellan's approach must have been terrifying. James Longstreet has described it. 'The blue uniforms of the Federals appeared among the trees that crowned the heights on the eastern bank of the Antietam. The number increased, and larger and larger grew the field of blue until it seemed to stretch as far as the eye could see, and from the tops of the mountains down to the edges of the stream gathered the great army of McClellan.' By any reasonable calculation Lee's army should have been totally destroyed. But incredibly it was still there at the end of the day. As Lee put it in his official report after the battle, 'Nothing could surpass the determined valor' with which the Confederate soldiers defeated every attempt to dislodge them from their positions. But nothing could surpass the incompetence of McClellan either as he failed to take advantage of the best chance for a complete Federal victory in the whole of the war. We have already seen how slow he was to come to battle. Once he arrived he did virtually nothing to prevent Jackson's men from Harper's Ferry reinforcing Lee. When he finally fought the battle he never made use of his overwhelming superiority in numbers. Two whole corps of fresh men were never used in the battle. The rest of his army were employed in three separate attacks on different parts of Lee's line which allowed Lee time to reinforce each threatened section with men who had not yet been in action.

As the dawn of 17 September came up cannon fire spread along both lines from left to right, across the creek and back again. To the thunder of the big guns was presently added the sharper rattling of musketry. The Confederates hastily ate their meagre breakfast and waited for the Federal onslaught. The first attack was led by Hooker on the left against Jackson. Jackson's men were thrown back in confusion but after being reinforced were able to counter-attack. This battle went on for several hours with enormous loss of life on both sides until Hooker's shattered divisions were finally withdrawn to recuperate. Instead of finishing off Jackson with a fresh attack

ABOVE Burnside's attack on the bridge was repulsed just in time by the arrival of Powell Hill. (Abby Aldrich Rockefeller Folk Art Collection)

ABOVE RIGHT The dead at Hagerstown Pike at Antietam. (Library of Congress)

McClellan now directed Sumner to move against D.H. Hill in the centre. This second stage of the battle was just as devastating as the first, many of the casualties being concentrated in a sunken road known as Bloody Lane that the Confederates were desperately defending. But once again McClellan did not push his advantage and Sumner withdrew. The final attack led by Burnside came on the Confederate right. For hours a bridge across the Antietam had been defended against enormous numbers by two regiments of Georgians. Finally about 4 pm the Federals broke through and crossed the bridge in force. It looked as though everything was lost as the

Confederates were forced farther and farther back and Lee no longer had fresh troops with which to reinforce them. Then, just at the critical moment, up came Powell Hill with some 4,000 men who had been marching from Harper's Ferry since half-past seven in the morning. They still had enough energy to counter-attack and the Federals were driven back across the river just as it began to get dark. The battle of the Antietam was over, some 23,000 men killed or wounded, Lee still on the west bank and McClellan on the east. Lee was still there on the next morning, but by nightfall he accepted the defeat of his invasion and took his shattered army back to Virginia.

5 Duel on the

Rappahannock

IF LEE FELT ANY DISAPPOINTMENT in this first serious check in his military career he did not show it. At first he was for recrossing the Potomac and invading Maryland all over again, but a closer look at his exhausted army convinced him that the time had come for rest and recuperation after the exertions of the summer. Fortunately, McClellan had no intention of disturbing Lee's rest. After one thrust forward had been parried by the Confederate rearguard he gave up all thought of pursuit and settled down to annoy Washington by doing nothing for several weeks.

Lee has been much criticised for his decision to fight at Sharpsburg. After the successful rearguard action at the passes through South Mountain he had plenty of time to escape from McClellan across the Potomac without risking his army against such overwhelming odds. The truth is that success had convinced Lee that he could always win, whatever the odds, and he challenged McClellan with the conviction that the Confederates would win the day. This may seem crazy, but when one considers how poorly the Federal commander managed the battle, it is possible to concede that Lee might well have been right to put so much faith in the ability of his troops and his divisional commanders to overcome their enemy. Lee realised earlier than most of the civil war generals that the advantage in warfare had now swung to the side of the defence. Men armed with rifles, well-entrenched in strong defensive positions with supporting artillery were very difficult to dislodge, except by surprise flanking movements. The men realised this too and there was no more criticism of orders to dig in – later veterans were to begin to dig in whenever they had a rest on the march. In his next two battles Lee was to demonstrate these new truths to the Federal generals, first by showing them how to defend a position and then how to turn an entrenched position by a flank attack. The only problem was that one day they might learn something from all the lessons he was teaching them.

Meanwhile the Army of the Potomac had won a strategic, if not a tactical victory at Sharpsburg. Lincoln had been waiting some time for anything that looked remotely like a victory to play a very important card. At last he had decided to issue a proclamation emancipating the slaves and now was the time to do it. Many people jeered at Lincoln's Emancipation Proclamation because it only freed slaves who were not in territory controlled by the Federals, and hence could not be

PREVIOUS PAGES The battle of Fredericksburg on the Rappahannock River. (Radio Times Hulton Picture Library)

120

An evening around the campfire in the Confederate camp. (Radio Times Hulton Picture Library)

enforced, except following further victories in the field. But it showed to the world that the war was now no longer merely a war to preserve the Union but was also a moral crusade. Southern hopes of European recognition receded, except among extreme optimists, while Southern determination to resist was much strengthened by the now open threat to their institutions. The war which had started in such a low key was now a revolutionary struggle in which it seemed no holds were to be barred.

Proclamations from Washington had little immediate effect on the life of the Army of Northern Virginia. Life was in fact very pleasant in Lee's rest camp set in the pastoral surroundings of the Shenandoah Valley. The harvest in the valley had been good and the men relaxed and were fed well, their numbers increasing daily as the barefoot stragglers returned to camp and wounded men recovered in the fine autumn weather. Morale, low after the battle, was soon restored when Jeb Stuart led another dashing cavalry raid right round McClellan's army and into southern Pennsylvania,

121

returning with information, over 1,000 fresh horses and hardly a man hurt. Later the irrepressible cavalry leader was to be seen at Lee's headquarters enjoying the music while his banjo-player serenaded the Southern chiefs.

Visitors were amazed at the lack of pomp in Lee's camp. He refused to make his headquarters in a house for fear of future reprisal on the owners and his tents were pitched in a rocky field. Everything was managed in a very calm and untheatrical way. There were no swarms of aides-de-camp dashing up and down, senior officers slept under waggons wrapped in blankets, no one from the general downward had more than the minimum of equipment and much of this equipment was stamped 'U.S.', demonstrating Southern ability to do without most of the supply problems which dominated the life of generals such as McClellan. In the centre of everything was Lee himself, calmly giving orders, writing letters, chatting with his staff and giving out an aura of confidence and unflappability. The secret of his control lay in the enormous respect his men had for him; the respect felt by children for a much-loved and admired father.

McClellan did nothing to disturb this idyll. Even a visit by Lincoln himself to his camp could do nothing to rouse him. As always he refused to move until everything down to the last minute piece of equipment was ready, and until he had several tens of thousands of reinforcements with which to do battle with the legions of Lee. But this time his caution was to lose him his job. McClellan at last started to move across the Potomac late in October, six weeks after the battle in which he had brought Lee to his knees, and then moved slowly south along the east side of Blue Ridge, seizing and holding the gaps in the ridge as he advanced. Lee sent Longstreet across the mountains to face him and left Jackson in the valley. But McClellan's progress was too slow for Lincoln. On 5 November he decided that he had had enough of the Young Napoleon and ordered him to turn over the command of the Army of the Potomac to General Ambrose E. Burnside. The farewell of McClellan, a great provider and a great protector of his troops, was a moving affair as the whole army cheered him and begged him to stay. Some indeed thought he might refuse to obey the President. But McClellan was not the sort of man who could march on Washington and lead a military *coup d'état* and he left quietly, disappearing from the war to his home in New Jersey.

122

Burnside, a close friend of McClellan's, had been reluctant to take command. A charming, friendly man with fantastic 'sideburns' and moustache, he had little military skill and knew it. Nevertheless his very first move caught Lee on the hop, something that McClellan had never managed to do. Feinting towards Longstreet at Culpeper near the mountains, he suddenly moved his whole force towards Fredericksburg, with almost indecent haste for the Federal army. Burnside's plan was to cross the Rappahannock and move rapidly towards Richmond. His first corps was at the river before Lee realised where he was headed and was able to order Longstreet to move east to oppose Burnside's crossing.

Unfortunately this initial burst of speed was the last praiseworthy thing that Burnside did on his whole campaign before he was in turn superseded, some three months after he took command. For, when he got to the Rappahannock, the pontoon bridges which he had ordered from Washington had not turned up. Instead of moving up the river, where there were several fords, he stayed opposite Fredericksburg, thus allowing Lee plenty of time to bring his whole army up to oppose him. December and cold weather arrived to find the two armies facing each other from strong positions each side of the river. Burnside's army was on Stafford Heights from where his artillery could cover the river, the town on the south side and the plain beyond it. Lee's men were on a range of hills on the other side of the river, firmly entrenched and no longer suffering from that deficiency in artillery which had been the fate of Confederate armies earlier in the war. Every battlefield had been carefully gleaned, both for guns and gun-metal from smashed pieces of artillery, and now Lee had over 250 cannon which could cover all approaches to his position.

Burnside's pontoon bridges eventually turned up and after various delays he started to try and cross the 140-yard wide river on 11 December. Despite constant bombardment of the town, Confederate sharp-shooters hidden in houses on the riverside were able to make life extremely unpleasant for the bridge-builders, but Burnside finally got his army across and was ready to assault Lee's position by dawn on 13 December. What followed was described by a Southern gunner as 'the simplest and easiest won battle of the war'.

The early morning of 13 December presented Lee's men, secure in their entrenchments on the hills behind Fredericksburg, with a magnificent spectacle. A dense fog overhung the

By 1863 war had scarred the
face of Virginia.
(British Museum)

whole of the plain beneath them, but they could hear the clank
and rattle of arms and the voices of the Union soldiers as they
got into position. A little later a light breeze sprang up, first
hardly moving the fog but then suddenly rolling it away to
reveal the whole of Burnside's vast army in the plain below.
Burnside then attempted to assault Lee's position, his two
main thrusts coming at two of the strongest places in the line.
Charge after charge was smashed into pieces by the artillery

and by infantry massed five deep in a sunken road behind a stone wall which provided ready-made cover for the defenders. No one could watch without at the same time being sickened by the carnage and full of admiration for the bravery of the Federal soldiers. Burnside destroyed a tenth of his army on that terrible December day and would have tried again the next day, leading the charge in person, if his corps commanders had not remonstrated with him. Standing at the top of the hill Lee watched the spectacle before him and made his famous remark: 'It is well that war is so terrible. We should grow too fond of it.'

Burnside recrossed the river and the two armies went into winter quarters facing each other. It was a cold winter with snow and sleet and unusable roads. Burnside tried once to move out of his position but this fiasco, appropriately called the Mud March, brought an end to his brief career as commander of the Army of the Potomac. Lincoln, having tried the man who failed to break the Confederate right at Sharpsburg, now decided to try the man who had failed to break the Confederate left. 'Fighting Joe' Hooker, intriguer, drinker and gambler took command. Lee, who was not impressed by his new opponent's nickname, normally referred to him as Mr F. J. Hooker.

The winter of 1862-3 was a hard one for the Army of Northern Virginia. They began to regret those greatcoats and blankets so blithely cast by the roadside in the previous summer. The blockade was much tighter now and supplies of clothing and food were very limited. Southern ladies continued to do what they could; more socks were knitted, marvellous patches appeared on the soldiers' ragged trousers, expensive carpets were cut up to be made into soldiers' blankets by the ladies of Richmond, but the truth was that the winter was hard for civilian as well as soldier. Prices in Richmond were soaring. Between 1860 and 1863 the price of flour rose $2\frac{1}{2}$ times, bacon 8 times, sugar 15 times and coffee was almost unobtainable. In April there was a riot in Richmond when a mob of hungry women attacking the stores had to be dispersed at bayonet point. The people looked like vagabonds, wearing dingy, dilapidated clothes, many with faces pale with hunger. Nearly everyone had relatives who had been killed or wounded and soon Richmond was to be a city of women in mourning where even the church bells had been melted down to be cast into cannon. Out in the country,

125

which the army was no longer able to control, things were even worse. Federal foragers and irregulars from both sides stripped farmhouses of everything, killing the animals, burning fences and emptying barns. The men were in the army and many of the slaves had run off, leaving women and children defenceless against the increasingly savage guerrilla bands. War was no longer quite the lark it had seemed early in 1861, but Richmond still thrilled to think that Lee's great army, still undefeated, lay between them and the enemy. 'All quiet on the Rappahannock' was welcome news that winter.

Lee's letters were a ray of comfort to the refugees in his own family. In October his much-loved daughter Annie died, but despite his grief he was still able to write entertaining letters to her sisters and mother. His daughter Mildred said that in Lee's letters 'one has glimpses of a great war raging mercilessly, while the chief actor sits down, to the sound of shot and cannon and pours out his heart in affection to his "little daughters".' A charming letter to another daughter Agnes provides a good example of his style.

General Hooker is obliged to do something: I do not know what it will be. He is playing the Chinese game, trying what frightening will do. He runs out his guns, starts his wagons and troops up and down the river, and creates an excitement generally. Our men look on in wonder, give a cheer, and all again subsides '*in status quo ante bellum*'. I wish you were here with me today. You would have to sit by this little stove, look out at the rain, and keep yourself dry. But here come, in all their wet, the adjutant-generals with the papers. I must stop and go to work. See how kind God is: we have plenty to do in good weather and bad. . . .

Lee saw his sons quite often for, excepting Custis, the eldest, who spent the war mostly in Richmond, they were serving in his own army. Rooney was in command of a brigade of cavalry while Rob, the youngest, was aide to his cousin Fitzhugh, another cavalry general.

Lee's letters both to his family and to the government in Richmond are full of concern for the plight of his soldiers, 'our poor bushmen' as he describes them to his wife. But busy and cold as they were they had the will to survive and enjoy themselves. Groups of soldiers built log huts to keep out the cold, experimented with novel cuisine, patched their clothes and amused themselves as we have seen by the curious antics of Mr F.J. Hooker. Every winter saw a great religious revival

So desperate was the Confederates' need for armaments that church bells were given to be melted down for cannon. (Library of Congress)

movements in the Confederate army as thousands, encouraged by the pious example of leaders such as Lee and Jackson, flocked to prayer meetings and sought salvation. The weather itself could provide entertainment and heavy snow found the whole army engaging in enormous snowball fights. Down on the picket lines the soldiers engaged in an unprecedented form of trading with the enemy, using model yachts to sail goods across the river. As one soldier describes it, 'The communication was almost constant and the vessels, many of them really beautiful little craft, with shapely hulls, nicely painted; elaborate rigging, trim sails, closed decks, and perfect working steering apparatus.... On a sunny, pleasant day the waters were fairly dotted with the fairy fleet.' The main items of exchange were newspapers and Southern tobacco for Northern coffee and sugar. Shouting and singing across the river, Johnny Reb and Billy Yank found that they had much in common, even if they were enemies.

But enemies they were and as spring came and the roads

128

Roasting corn.
Camp on the road.

Federal troops occupy a
Southern home; part of
'Old Westover Mansion',
by E.L.Henry. (In the
collection of the Corcoran
Gallery)

The Confederate army passed the winter in snowball fighting, religious revivals and trading with the enemy. (The Bettmann Archive; Library of Congress; British Museum)

began to dry out the two great armies started to come to life again. Lee remained on the defensive with his cavalry watching the fords, but Hooker had to destroy Lee's army if he did not want to follow in the steps of Burnside and McClellan. Fighting Joe was a very confident man and boasted, 'I have the finest army the sun ever shone on. My plans are perfect, and when I start to carry them out, may God have mercy on General Lee, for I will have none!' What were these plans which made Hooker crow so?

In fact Hooker's plan was a very good one, worthy of Lee himself, and if he had not lost his nerve at a crucial point he might well have destroyed the Confederate army. He planned to divide his army of some 120,000 into two, each half being as big as the whole of Lee's force. One half was to march west along the Rappahannock and crossing by several fords make its way through a great area of dense woodland known as the Wilderness to emerge on Lee's left flank. The rest of the army under Sedgwick was to remain on the heights opposite Fredericksburg until Lee was forced from his position. The two halves were then to crush him between them. Prior to his flanking movement nearly the whole of Hooker's cavalry, some 10,000 men under Stoneman, were to ride round Lee's army destroying his communications and his main supply depot at Hanover Junction. Since Lee himself was expecting Hooker to use his water communications to attack from the peninsula, the Federals had a good chance to surprise.

The first thing to go wrong was that the cavalry did not get off on its raid until Hooker's flanking infantry had already moved up towards the fords. Nevertheless he sent them off, better late than never, and they disappeared from sight and out of the campaign. Stoneman was no Stuart and Lee was largely able to ignore him. Meanwhile Hooker left himself with virtually no cavalry. For all that, his flank movement got off to a good start in complete secrecy and it was not till late on 28 April 1863 when the leading men were actually crossing the fords, in some places wading up to their armpits in the icy water, that Lee realised what was happening and even then he did not know the strength of the movement. Lee had other problems. Longstreet had been sent off on a detachment with two whole divisions and, despite a request for his return, Lee's independent-minded 'war horse' never turned up for the Battle of Chancellorsville in which Lee was to be so heavily outnumbered.

134

Once Lee learned of the flanking movement he sent Anderson with a division to hold the road leading from the Wilderness to Fredericksburg, while he decided where he thought the main thrust was coming from. By 30 April the momentum of Hooker's flank movement had completely broken down. His leading corps commanders were all ready to move against Lee's left, but Hooker had lost his nerve and decided to entrench himself in the Wilderness itself where he felt certain he could destroy Lee if he should come out. In so short time he had completely lost the initiative. 'Fighting Joe' would not come out to fight! Unkind observers blamed Hooker's behaviour on the fact that he had recently given up drinking. If he had only had a few drinks to steady his nerve or got so drunk that command devolved on someone else then the campaign might have been a success.

The place where Hooker had decided to stand was hardly suitable for a big battle. The Wilderness was an area of about one hundred square miles of dense thickets of pine and oak south of the Rappahannock. Visibility was virtually nil. An important road ran east and west through the forest and there were several lesser roads linking this main road to the fords and going out of the forest on the southern side. Right in the middle of the Wilderness was an important cross-roads and here lay the imposing white-columned mansion called Chancellorsville. This was Hooker's headquarters. As a place to fight it had many disadvantages. Manoeuvre was nearly impossible and there was very little scope for the Federals to make use of their advantage in artillery.

Hooker's halt gave Lee's scouts time to find out where nearly all the Federal army was, and by the evening of 30 April Lee was able to plan his counter-offensive. It was a typical Lee plan. The rheumatic and irascible general Jubal Early was left with 10,000 men and considerable artillery to hold the heights above Fredericksburg against his old West Point class-mate Sedgwick who originally had 60,000. 'Deserters' were fed in to Sedgwick's army to leak the information that Longstreet's two divisions had returned from detachment. Although Lee could hardly feel too confident about Early's position, the experience of 13 December indicated that Sedgwick would have quite a job to storm the heights and come to Hooker's assistance. Meanwhile Jackson, with the whole of the rest of his army numbering some 45,000 men, went to face Hooker's 60,000 at Chancellorsville. By the

135

evening of 1 May the two armies, marching towards each other along the road that went through the Wilderness towards Fredericksburg, clashed and positions were taken up for the night facing each other through the trees. Lee, having organised Early's position, rode up to the Wilderness to consult with Jackson. A wave of cheers greeted Lee as he rode up and one old soldier described Lee's reaction. 'He lifted his hat, taking it by the crown with his right hand and holding it suspended above his majestic head. I remember, too, how the men greeted him, shouting, "What a head, what a head! See that glorious head! God bless it, God bless it!"'

Many descriptions have been given of this last meeting of the two great soldiers. Lee and Jackson sat on biscuit boxes in the moonlit pine woods and Lee asked his gaunt lieutenant, 'How can we get at these people?' Jackson outlined what he had discovered of the enemy's position. To the front the Federals were well placed, their trenches protected by breastworks and the bush cleared for one hundred yards to their front to give firing room. The enemy's left was firmly fixed on the river. But what of his right? Just then Jeb Stuart rode up in the moonlight with momentous news. His men had discovered that the Federal right was completely unprotected. Lee's and Jackson's faces lit up. There just had to be a road which went round to the enemy's right. Jackson rose, touched his cap and said, 'My troops will move at four o'clock.'

Before dawn of the next day, 2 May, there was great excitement as various local residents and soldiers with local knowledge, including a chaplain in Jackson's corps, provided the information that enabled Jackson to work out a twelve-mile route to put him beyond the Federal right. But time was getting on and it was not till 7.30 that the head of Jackson's column of 32,000 men set off, leaving Lee with only 13,000 to face Hooker who had now been reinforced to over five times Lee's numbers. But Lee remained quite calm as Jackson rode off, and instructed his men to keep Hooker busy with artillery fire and powerful skirmishing. All day his ears were strained to hear the sound of Jackson's guns as they attacked the Federal right, nearly five miles away.

Jackson's route lay south and south-west till he was at a road junction some five miles direct from Chancellorsville. Then he turned to the north and north-west for about five miles until he could get his men on a line facing east ready to attack Hooker's right flank. The Federals saw Jackson as he was

Lee and Jackson in council on the night before Chancellorsville. (Anne S. K. Brown Military Collection)

moving south and thought he was retreating. A weak attempt was made at his rearguard and then he seemed to be forgotten. How badly Hooker needed his cavalry, gallivanting miles to the south that day.

Although this flank march is perhaps the most famous of all Jackson's marches he did not make very good time and this fact was to spoil his move of much of its potential success. Such slowness was hardly Jackson's fault. He urged the men on continuously, 'press forward, press forward', placing guards of strong men with fixed bayonets behind each regiment to prevent straggling. The weather was warm and the men felt very hot with the dense woods on each side depriving them of air and all were hungry and thirsty by the end of the march. But it was not till after five o'clock that Jackson's line was in place and ready to attack. He placed his men in three lines about two miles long, on both sides of the turnpike leading to Chancellorsville, just over three miles away.

Guarding Hooker's right flank was the Federal 11th Corps comprised largely of Germans and commanded by the one-armed general Howard. Before the attack Jackson was led to a vantage point by Lee's nephew, the cavalry general Fitz Lee.

Below and but a few hundred yards distant ran the Federal line of battle. There was the line of defence, with abatis in front and long lines of stacked arms in rear. Two cannons were visible in the part of the line seen. The soldiers were in groups in the rear, laughing, chatting and smoking, probably engaged here and there in games of cards and other amusements indulged in while feeling safe and comfortable, awaiting orders. In the rear of them were other parties driving up and butchering beeves.

It was a scene of great calm.

At a quarter past five Jackson moved forward. Soon he ran into Federal skirmishers and the bugles blew the charge. Sweating, tearing their clothes on thickets and driving all the animals of the forest before them, Jackson's men charged forward screaming and firing. Howard's corps simply disintegrated before the onslaught, threw their rifles away and ran into the dense thickets. Nothing could stop Jackson's men and he routed line after line. Slowly some order appeared in the other Federal forces and a stand was made just west of the Chancellorsville cross-roads where the out-generalled Hooker had been sitting on the verandah of his headquarters as the first terrified fugitives came running past. Now Jackson's men were slowing up. Darkness was falling and the tired but exhilarated soldiers were at last brought to a halt.

Just after nine in the evening Jackson rode forward to reconnoitre the confused position at the front where Federal and Confederate were now hopelessly entangled in the forest. It was a cloudy night with occasional breaks which allowed the moon to illuminate the dramatic scene. There was a moment of silence and then a volley was fired from the woods as Confederate soldiers mistook their general's party for Federal scouts. Jackson wheeled his horse in front of another portion of his own men and bullets from a second volley wounded him in three places. Jackson, bleeding heavily, fell and was taken from the battlefield. Almost immediately his entourage was hit by a Federal bombardment and his second-in-command Powell Hill was also wounded. This was a bad time for such

138

The Confederate charge at Hooker's troops, 3 May 1863. (Anne S.K. Brown Military Collection)

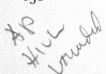

A corps of the Confederate
army marching by night
through the burning woods.
(Radio Times Hulton
Picture Library)

a disaster, especially as Jackson always kept his plans to himself. The cavalry commander Jeb Stuart was brought up to take command of Jackson's men.

Lee got the news of Jackson's wound at midnight, but did not realise how bad it was. Nevertheless it took most of the joy out of the day's victory. And now it was time to think of the morning. He got a message through to Stuart telling him to make the junction of the two wings of the army his first aim on the next day. Hooker, who had been reinforced in the evening and now had nearly double the numbers of the Confederates, obligingly helped Lee to reunite his army. He ordered the Federal corps thrust between Lee's two wings to withdraw, their position being immediately seized by Stuart and crowned with artillery to enfilade the rest of the Federals. This was not Hooker's only mistake. He made no attempt to attack Stuart's very vulnerable left flank with the 30,000 men in Meade's and Reynolds's corps who were ideally placed between the Confederate left wing and the river. All that he did was to order Sedgwick to attack at Fredericksburg and come in on Lee's rear. He would not attack himself until Sedgwick's arrival!

While Stuart was attacking from the west, Anderson had been working his way up through the rough, wooded country to the south. By ten o'clock Lee's two wings were reunited for the final thrust to clear the cross-roads. Lee, up front with the soldiers as they fought their way through the woods, rode up to the burning mansion that had been Hooker's headquarters. A great cheer met him from the soldiers, their faces black with the smoke of battle. All around the woods were in flames. Hooker had retreated and the battle was won. It was one of Lee's greatest triumphs.

But there was still more to be done. That same Sunday morning another battle was going on at Fredericksburg ten miles away. Sedgwick had crossed over the river and attacked Early's left and right with little success. Then he gathered his men together and determined to attack his centre, the very place where the enormous slaughter had taken place in the battle of 13 December. In order to make sure that no momentum was lost as his men loaded to return the Confederate fire he directed the front ranks to carry unloaded rifles with fixed bayonets. This suicide charge carried the day. Despite heavy losses, the momentum of the Federal charge carried them over the wall, across the sunken road and up the hill beyond. In a

quarter of an hour the position that had previously resisted
attack after attack had fallen and Early's men fled the field.
But Sedgwick had no cavalry with which to pursue him.

Lee, when he heard the news of Early's defeat, once again
divided his army. Leaving Stuart to hold Hooker's dispirited
force, he marched back with McLaws's and Anderson's divisions to resist Sedgwick's advance. A good defensive position
was taken up at Salem Church on a wooded ridge some four
miles from Stuart's right. That evening the battle raged back
and forth till dark. Sedgwick passed a restless night and the
next day found himself in a wedge. Early had regrouped his
men and come up behind him. Slowly Sedgwick was forced
north to the river and in the darkness of the early morning of
5 May he crossed over to the north bank. That same day
Hooker also retreated across the river. Lee was robbed once
again of total victory and it is one of the few blots on his
campaign that Hooker's vast and beaten army were able

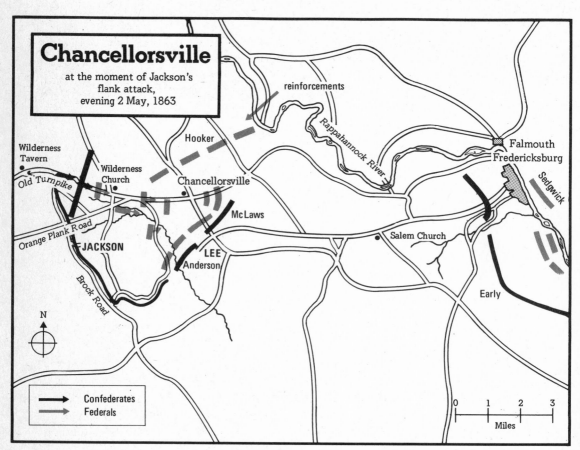

Chancellorsville

at the moment of Jackson's
flank attack,
evening 2 May, 1863

A Federal battery in the second battle of Fredericksburg, 3 May 1863. (Radio Times Hulton Picture Library)

[handwritten marginalia: "Sum of battle Lee's greatest win"]

to cross a swollen river without detection by the cavalry.

Chancellorsville is normally regarded as Lee's greatest battle. The defeat of an army over twice his size was a quite remarkable feat, as was the daring of dividing his army to send Jackson on his famous flank march. But the cost was very heavy. The Confederate casualties in the battles at Chancellorsville and in Early's fight at Fredericksburg were 10,000, nearly a fifth of his whole army. The defeated and out-generalled Hooker lost 14,000, a far smaller proportion of his army and he could raise more men far more easily than Lee. What is more Lee lost his great lieutenant. Jackson, the 'great and good', whose arm was amputated when he was carried out of the battle, died of pneumonia on 10 May. His body lay in state at Richmond wrapped in the Confederate flag and covered with lilies of the valley and other spring flowers. Later he was buried in the Valley of Virginia where a year earlier he had first astonished the world by his extraordinary military skills. His last words were: 'Let us cross over the river and rest under the shade of the trees.'

145

6 The Turn of the Tide

THE DAY AFTER JACKSON'S DEATH Lee wrote to his son Custis in Richmond asking for 'my gray sack, cotton drawers, and some cotton socks that I sent down last fall'. The weather was once again getting hot and it was time to exchange his winter gear for some summer things. It was also time to start thinking about his summer campaign. The defeat of Hooker had given Lee the initiative and it was obvious that he, like Jackson, must cross over the river, but it was also clear that he would be able to expect little rest when he reached the other side.

Before he could move forward, however, he must reorganise the army. There was no one capable of commanding half the army in battle as Jackson had, so Lee decided to divide his force up into three corps of three divisions each. The First Corps was given to Longstreet, now back from detachment with dangerous ideas of his own importance. At times it seems he thought he was Lee's equal, if not his superior, and he was always ready to give his opinion of what should be done. Unfortunately his ideas on both strategy and tactics rarely squared with those of Lee and there were to be times when Longstreet exhibited a sulkiness close to rank disobedience in

executing orders in which he had no faith. For all that, he was the best corps commander that Lee had and there was no alternative but to rely on his 'old war horse', as he chose to call him. The Second Corps, composed mainly of Jackson's old troops, was given to Stonewall's favourite divisional commander Dick Ewell. 'Baldy' Ewell was an extraordinary looking man, with bulging eyes and a wild moustache. A middle-aged extrovert, hard-riding and hard-swearing, he had fought extremely well in the Valley Campaign and at the Second Battle of Bull Run where he had lost a leg. But there were some who were not sure about his recent behaviour. His marriage late in life to the Widow Brown appeared to have made him soft. The Third Corps went to the fiery Powell Hill, perhaps the man with the best combat record in the army but untested at such a high rank. It was, then, with a new team that Lee set forth on what turned out to be the most disastrous campaign of his career. He made no change in his method of handling senior officers. As before he outlined the broad plan and left them to implement it as seemed best. And, as before, he tended to leave them with extremely vague orders. Lee's letters to his generals teem with expressions like 'if you

Lee's bad habit

think proper', 'if practicable' or 'I think you had better'. Such wording worked very well with a Jackson, but he had no Jacksons now, and although he always hoped a new Jackson might spring forth from the army, he hoped in vain.

As in the summer of 1862 Lee was firmly committed to an advance. The reasoning behind his decision was much the same as before. An advance into Union territory would solve his supply problems, enabling his army to subsist at the enemy's expense while the Virginian harvest was safely garnered to his rear. Lee had no illusions about being able to stay long in the Union or even taking any of the great cities. But his mere presence would once more have a great impact on public opinion, an impact which would have all the more effect if he could win a great battle in Pennsylvania. Southern hopes had been much raised in the previous winter when the Democrats made great gains in senatorial and gubernatorial elections. More military victories could push opinion even further against the Republicans – after all Lincoln himself had only eighteen months before he came up for re-election. And of course there was always English recognition, that Southern pot of gold to dream about, though the Emancipation Proclamation had done much to damn the South in English eyes. Finally, invasion might take some pressure off the west where, after a long stalemate, affairs were once more going against the Confederacy. All eyes were turned on Vicksburg, the last Southern stronghold on the Mississippi, which now seemed to be doomed as Grant, in one of the finest campaigns of the whole war, tightened his grip on the powerfully defended river port.

Jefferson Davis had complete faith in Lee, the only one of his generals who won conclusive victories. But his faith was not strong enough to let Lee have reinforcements. The President's eyes were rarely far from the map and the evidence it gave of the number of different places in which Federal naval power might land troops to invade the Confederacy. Pins marked these places and other pins marked contingents of veteran soldiers drawn from the armies in the field to defend them. In vain did Lee argue that his own invasion and the diseases carried by the summers of the Deep South would bring the Federal troops back to defend the Union. The defensive-minded Davis, supported by the frightened governors of the states of the Deep South, would not let Lee have another man and even threatened to strip his already

OPPOSITE The Federal ordnance was amply supplied by the industrialised North. (Brady Collection, Library of Congress)

150

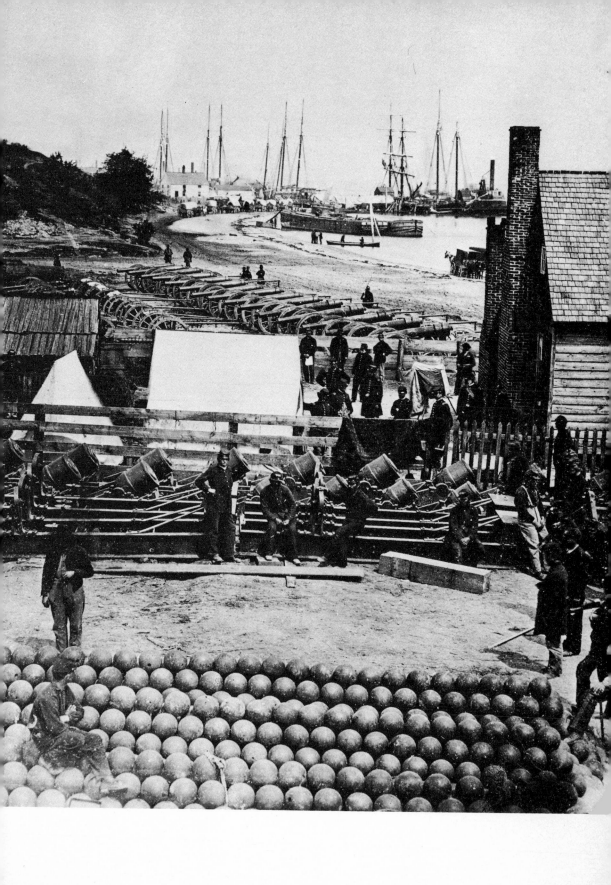

small army of further men to man these scattered defences.

The truth of the matter was of course that there were just not enough men in the South to deal with every emergency. Casualties, desertion and evasion of conscription had already taken their toll of the available man-power. Somebody had to work the few munitions factories, keep the railways going, supervise agriculture and run the government. To the soldiers facing danger in the field it seemed that there were far too many people in such protected occupations. But in truth there were far too few. The Southern railways were falling to pieces under the heavy traffic of the war and most of the pre-war maintenance men were in the Confederate army or were Yankees who had gone home at the first sign of trouble. The supply of munitions was better than it had been at the beginning of the war, but was still nowhere like as good as that in the North, where capitalist forces now released by the flood of government demand were pouring out fantastic quantities of uniforms, guns and ammunition. And all the time the Federal blockade became stronger, denying to the Confederates the possibility of imports from Europe to make up their deficiencies. The most important deficiency – men – could never be made up. Recruiting had just about dried up completely, while Lincoln at every set-back was able to call for another hundred thousand men or so.

However, even if Lee's army was rather small for an invasion, it was in superb condition and extremely confident of its ability to beat anything and anyone that Lincoln might send out to challenge it. We have fairly impartial reports from the stream of English journalists and soldiers who followed Lee's army as they might a successful football team. One of the best of these writers, Lieutenant-Colonel Fremantle of the Coldstream Guards, travelled with Lee on his advance into the Union and reported that 'At no period of the war have the men been so well equipped, so well clothed, so eager for a fight, or so confident of success – a very different state of affairs from that which characterised the Maryland invasion of last year, when half of the army were barefooted stragglers. . . .' By now virtually all the infantry were armed with rifles and the artillery, though still not as well-equipped as their opponents, were certainly formidable as had been demonstrated at Fredericksburg. The only arm which seemed to have been actually run down since the beginning of the war was the cavalry. In 1861 an enthusiastic cavalryman from Virginia had

152

boasted that 'every horse, like its rider, had a strain of gentle blood.' Throughout the first two years of the war the Confederate cavalry, for the most part riding horses from their own homes, had completely outclassed their opponents. But hard riding had not done their almost irreplaceable mounts much good and the Federal cavalry had rapidly been catching up in numbers, equipment and horsemanship. Shortly before Lee set off to invade Pennsylvania, the Federal cavalry had surprised Jeb Stuart at Brandy Station and the flamboyant general had only been able to extract his men from the battle after suffering many casualties, including Lee's son, Rooney. Stuart's pride took a heavy knock in this affair and his attempt to regain his reputation was to have very serious results for the safety of Lee's army.

good V.O. —

Lee had decided to invade down the Shenandoah Valley, crossing the Potomac above Harper's Ferry and then continuing north across Maryland into Pennsylvania, keeping the South Mountains between him and the Federal army. This area of western Pennsylvania was very fertile and would provide the subsistence and stores which was one of the major reasons for the advance. Throughout the campaign Lee maintained strict discipline, refusing to allow his men to pillage in reprisal for Federal depredations in Virginia.

Muskets from the Civil War.
(Museum of
the Confederacy)

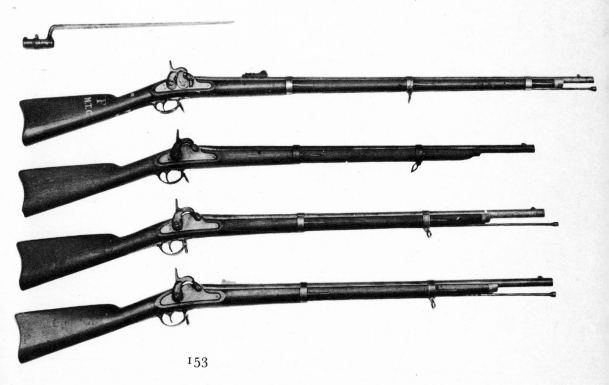

153

Horses, cattle and foodstuffs were to be commandeered and paid for only by properly accredited supply officers. Even the Pennsylvanians paid grudging tribute to the good behaviour of the Confederate army, though they can hardly have seen much difference between pillaging and payment in the worthless Confederate money. Lee himself was happy with his men's forebearance, except for a few cases of what he was pleased to describe as 'forgetfulness', and congratulated them in a circular issued later in the campaign which illustrated the philosophy behind his orders.

It must be remembered that we make war only upon armed men, and that we cannot take vengeance for the wrongs our people have suffered without lowering ourselves in the eyes of all whose abhorrence has been excited by the atrocities of our enemies, and offending against Him to whom vengeance belongeth, without whose favour and support our efforts must all prove in vain.

The advance was headed by Ewell's corps who set off towards the Valley on 10 June. The speed and determination which he demonstrated on his way north excited much admiration and many thought that the bald man with the wooden leg must indeed be a second Jackson. By the end of the month he had cleared the Federals out of the Valley, moved rapidly through Maryland and southern Pennsylvania and was near Harrisburg, the state capital, two hundred miles from his starting point. Longstreet's corps remained east of Blue Ridge to guard the passes and Hill stayed on at Fredericksburg to block a possible Federal advance on Richmond. Hooker indeed wanted to do just this, but was informed that his job was to protect Washington and attack Lee's army. At one point this army was spread out all the way from Pennsylvania to Fredericksburg, a tempting morsel, but the now dispirited general never attacked and soon retired to the Manassas area.

As soon as Hooker started withdrawing Hill and Longstreet started to follow Ewell down the Valley, leaving Jeb Stuart and the main body of the cavalry on the other side of Blue Ridge to guard the passes and keep Lee informed of the movements of Hooker's army. For the one time in his dashing career Stuart was to let Lee down. Anxious to regain the reputation tarnished at Brandy Station, Stuart decided to ride round the Federal army as he had twice ridden round McClellan. But the Federal withdrawal into Maryland kept Hooker's army between Stuart and Lee. It was not till 2 July that Stuart's tired troopers on their worn-out horses were able to fight their way round the head of the Federal army and rejoin the units they were supposed to be protecting and feeding with information. During this time Lee's army has been well described as a 'blindfold giant', advancing into the Union with no idea where the Federal army was. Lee had other cavalry, mostly irregulars from western Virginia, but these were naturally engaged in other activities and in any case had no leader as skilled in interpreting information as Jeb Stuart.

As Longstreet and Hill advanced down the Shenandoah and into Maryland in the wake of Ewell they met a stream of drovers moving south. These men were taking back to Virginia the spoils of Pennsylvania, collected and paid for with Confederate money by the men of Ewell's corps and by Jenkins's irregular cavalry who rode with Ewell as official foragers. The road was crowded with waggons and horses and droves of cattle and sheep. As Lee rode north he knew that at least one aspect of his campaign, perhaps the most important, was going to be a success. There would be meat and horses in Virginia that winter. As he established his headquarters in Chambersburg, Pennsylvania, this was some consolation for the continued silence from Stuart which was beginning to worry him.

Pennsylvania was real enemy territory to the Confederates, made more foreign by the incomprehensible accents of the 'Pennsylvania Dutch' who lived there. These farmers made it clear that they were interested only in farming and had no interest in who won the war. They just wanted to be left alone and watched the advance of the Confederate army with sullen indifference. They naturally resented the removal of their livestock, which prevented them tilling their fields, but except for a few outspoken women in the towns they did nothing to oppose the invasion. The Southerners found the country fertile but dull and were amazed at the small size of the fields and the large size of the barns. A cavalry officer on Longstreet's staff summed up Confederate reactions to this strange country. 'We are surrounded by enemies and black looks, Dutchmen and big barns.'

Lee's well-disciplined stripping of the Pennsylvania countryside was rudely interrupted on 28 June when a scout brought in two pieces of information. Hooker had been replaced as commander of the Army of the Potomac by one of his corps commanders, General George Meade, a competent but uninspiring soldier who had fought well at Fredericksburg. More seriously, the Federal army had crossed the Potomac and were marching north and north-east from Frederick, Maryland. Misled by Stuart's silence, Lee had thought that they were still in Virginia. Once convinced of the truth of the scout's information Lee acted fast. He must reunite his army, at present scattered over fifty miles of country, and then find Meade to bring him to battle. Orders were sent to all corps commanders to move east of the mountains and assemble in the Cashtown-Gettysburg region.

Lee's orders had set his army on a collision course with the Federal army. The small town of Gettysburg, so soon to be world-famous, was chiefly remarkable for being the meeting-point of ten roads. Ewell's scattered corps were now moving down three of these roads from the north and north-east. Lee with the main Confederate army was moving east from Chambersburg. Meade's army was advancing along three different roads from the south. Neither general particularly wanted to fight at that particular time at Gettysburg, but neither had sufficiently good reconnaissance to give him much choice. It was a classic example of what military men call a 'meeting engagement'.

The Englishman, Colonel Fremantle, travelling from Chambersburg on the road to Gettysburg with Longstreet's corps, first heard firing from the east at two in the afternoon of 1 July. At three he met wounded men and prisoners being taken away from the battlefield. At half-past four he came in sight of Gettysburg and joined generals Lee and Hill on the ridge to the west of the town. Looking across the town he could see the Federals retreating up a ridge on the other side of the valley, pursued by the Confederates with loud yells. What had happened was that the night before, the leading brigade of Hill's leading division had clashed to the west of the town with Federal dismounted cavalrymen, the leaders of Meade's army. On the following day the fighting had developed as more and more of the two armies turned up from all directions. Federal resistance had finally broken with the arrival of Early's division of Ewell's corps from the north. As a gunner engaged in the fight put it, 'We drove the enemy pell-mell over rolling wheat fields, through a grove, across a creek, up a little slope and into the town itself.' What Fremantle had seen was the end of this rout, as two Federal corps were chased out of the town and up on to the ridge to the south where defensive positions had already been prepared by a far-sighted Federal general. At this stage of the battle Lee had the initiative and more men in the immediate area of Gettysburg than the Federals. Sensing his chance to win a really decisive victory, Lee suggested to Ewell that he should assault the ridge where the enemy had fled. But he only suggested it. Ewell decided his men were too tired and the enemy too strong. The only real chance for Lee to win the battle of Gettysburg had gone. As the gunner who has just been quoted remarked, 'The tide, which taken at the flood might have led on to overwhelming victory and even to independence, had ebbed away forever.' Ewell had just shown that he was no second Jackson.

The battlefield of Gettysburg is distinguished by two parallel ridges running north and south. On the west is Seminary Ridge, so called because of the Lutheran Theological Seminary on its crest whose cupola provided a useful observation post. About three-quarters of a mile of orchards and cultivated fields separated this ridge, which was held by Lee, from Cemetery Ridge, the Federal position. The north end of this ridge was called Cemetery Hill, up which Colonel Fremantle had seen the defeated Federals running for their lives. East and south-east from Cemetery Hill the ridge turned back on itself to culminate in Culp's Hill. Due south from Cemetery Hill the ridge ran for some two miles to terminate in two boulder-strewn outcrops connected by a saddle, known as Little Round Top and Round Top. Lee's army were spread out in an inverted J facing the Federal position. The object of the battle was quite simple – to storm and seize the ridge held by Meade. Many attempts were made to do this: all of them failed and three days later what was left of the Army of Northern Virginia went home, having suffered its first serious defeat.

From the Confederate point of view the battle is characterised by a whole series of mistakes and delays, most of them chargeable to individual shortcomings. Not one of the Southern leaders was at the peak of his form on the first three bloody days of July 1863. Ewell appeared to have lost his nerve, Hill was sick, Stuart was absent without leave, and Longstreet was at his sulkiest. Disapproving of Lee's plans, he did his no doubt unintentional best to wreck them by inexplicable delays. As for Lee, the best that can be said was that every great general must have a bad day. His fault lay in

OVERLEAF The Confederates charge up Cemetery Hill at the battle of Gettysburg. 2 July 1863. (Anne S.K. Brown Military Collection)

157

doing nothing to galvanise his subordinates into action. One observer described his conduct on the crucial second day of the battle. 'Generally he sat quite alone on the stump of a tree. What I remarked especially was, that during the whole time the firing continued, he only sent one message and only received one report. It is evidently his system to arrange the plan thoroughly with the three corps commanders, and then leave to them the duty of modifying and carrying it out to the best of their abilities.'

This is exactly what Lee did do and the result was defeat. We have seen already that nothing could be done on the first day to excite Ewell into following up the Federal rout. For twenty-four hours from the end of this fight on 1 July Federal troops were coming up to Cemetery Ridge from the south-east to take their places in defensive positions on its crest. In the end the whole ridge was held in force. But on the evening of 1 July neither Culp's Hill nor the Round Tops were occupied. If the Confederates had moved fast at this early stage of the battle these hills could have been taken and crowned with artillery to enfilade the rest of the Federal position. Unfortunately for the cause of the South Gettysburg was not to be distinguished by such rapid thinking and action. Assaults on the Federal line were to be delayed sufficiently to allow Meade to mass his defences and ensure their failure.

On the second day of the battle Lee planned to send forward two simultaneous assaults to attack the Federal right and left, 'as early in the day as possible'. In the end the attacks were neither simultaneous nor early. Hour after hour passed and nothing happened until by late afternoon people began to wonder whether there was going to be a fight at all that day. Then, at last, unsupported by Ewell on the left, Longstreet's corps went into action at 4.30. His task was far harder than it would have been if he had set off at the right time. All Meade's army had by now arrived and one corps had been thrust forward into the no-man's land between the two ridges. It was here amongst peach orchards and wheat fields that the severest fighting of the day took place, as the Confederates slowly pushed the Federal soldiers back to the ridge line. But by the time that this had happened Longstreet's men were too tired to carry the ridge. As one of Lee's staff caustically remarked, 'After a severe conflict for several hours, Longstreet had gained the position which he could have occupied earlier in the day without opposition.' On the extreme right of Long-

160

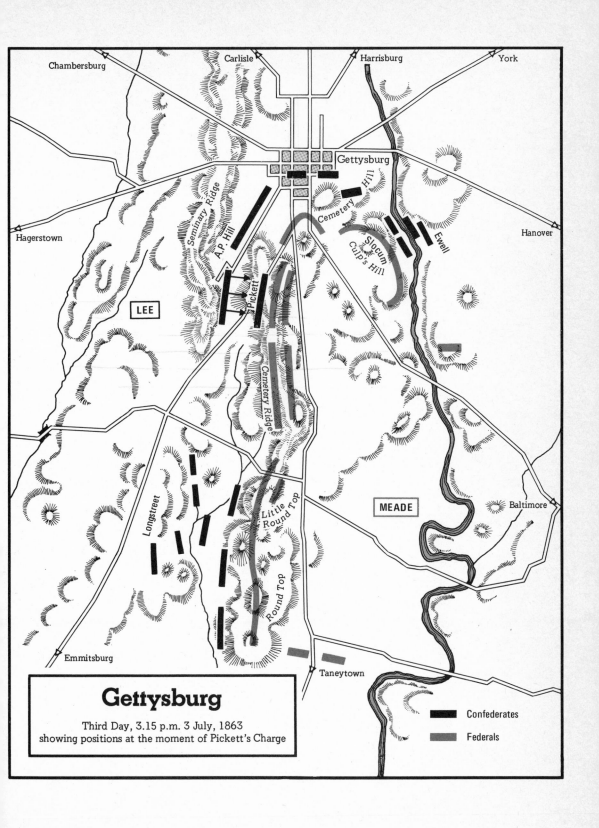

Gettysburg

Third Day, 3.15 p.m. 3 July, 1863
showing positions at the moment of Pickett's Charge

Confederates
Federals

street's line there was great excitement as Hood's division, many of them Texans, made a dash through the rough boulders which covered the steep slope of Little Round Top. For some reason this crucial hill was not occupied by the Federals at the beginning of Longstreet's advance, and the struggle developed into a race won by a Federal brigade who reached the crest just in time to force the Texans back as they swarmed on to the top in triumph. About sunset, after the battle on the Confederate right had finished, what was supposed to have been a simultaneous attack from the left began. Johnson's division of Ewell's corps assaulted Culp's Hill. Like Hood's men, the famous Louisiana Tigers nearly took the crest, only to be forced back as darkness fell.

Having failed to overcome the Federal defences on the left and right, Lee planned a final forlorn attack for the third day of the battle on the Federal centre. As before this was supposed to have been supported by an attack from the left. But this time the Federals took the initiative, restarting the battle against Johnson's division on Culp's Hill long before Lee's assault troops were ready to attack the centre. This battle on the left raged fiercely till eleven o'clock when the Federals were finally able to clear the hill, and the crack troops of Ewell's corps, Jackson's old Stonewall Brigade, had to accept the fact that they had met their match.

For two hours there was a comparative calm on the field. Meade was having lunch with his staff when at one o'clock two shots signalled the beginning of the most devastating bombardment yet seen in the war. For two hours the Federals hugged the ground on the central section of the ridge as 120 guns tried to blast them and their artillery to oblivion. But in fact the guns were firing just a little too high and little damage had been done when the Confederate artillery commander begged the assault troops to come quickly as his ammunition was running out.

There was a moment of silence before General George Pickett, curly-haired and 'altogether rather a desperate character', led his 15,000 men from Longstreet's and Hill's corps out of the shelter of the woods on Seminary Ridge where they had been sweltering in the heat all day. They made a magnificent spectacle as they moved eastward across the shallow valley in perfect formation with colours flying. The Federal guns held their fire until the line reached the road about half-way between the two ridges. Much slaughter was done as the Southerners hurriedly climbed the fences on each side of the road but still the line came on. As they got nearer, the Federal guns changed from shell to canister, tearing great holes in the line. But with parade-ground calm the ranks closed up and continued to advance. At last the Federal fire began to take its toll. The left wavered and then fell back. The right was taken in flank by Federal infantrymen pulled from the ridge. But the gallant centre, mainly Pickett's own division of Virginians, was still coming on. For more than half a mile they had been under constant fire with no chance of retaliating, but now they were close enough to return the fire. One volley into the Federal defence, then the bloodcurdling rebel yell and the survivors ran for the ridge. Federal resistance in their immediate front disappeared, but as Pickett looked round the top of the ridge he had temporarily gained he saw he could never hold the position. From all sides troops were crowding in on him. He had no choice but to take the lonely road back to where he had come from. The English observers, frantically looking for a good place to watch the fun, managed to miss the most dramatic spectacle in American military history and arrived at a suitable eminence only to see the dejected survivors of Pickett's division making their sad way back to the safety of the woods on Seminary Ridge. Lee hastened to console Pickett, almost hysterical at the destruction of his division. 'Come, General Pickett,' he said soothingly, 'this has been my fight and upon my shoulders rests the blame. The men and officers of your command have written the name of Virginia today as high as it has ever been written before.'

The Battle of Gettysburg had ended and Lee had failed. Each side suffered about 20,000 casualties, and later that year Mr Lincoln was to make a celebrated Address when he dedicated a cemetery to receive some of the corpses now scattered all over the field. But Lee could not wait that long. He ordered his dead to be buried and the wounded to be placed in waggons and ambulances and set on the road back to Virginia, while he waited for Meade's expected counter-attack. It never came and on the night of 4 July Lee withdrew his army and marched back through the mountains and then turned south towards the Potomac. The retreat was orderly and Meade offered little resistance, but at the last moment it seemed as if Lee's army was to be caught in a trap and exterminated. For, when he arrived at the river, he found that

BELOW A prisoner's record of life at
the Federal prison camp, Point
Lookout. (Maryland Historical Society)
OPPOSITE ABOVE A Northern view of
Confederate prisoners, representing
them as ragged hillbillies. (British
Museum) BELOW Three Southern
prisoners after Gettysburg. (Brady
Collection, Library of Congress)

. POINT LOOKOUT MD .

Nº 1. Boys that's my rat if you kill him, he been eating my bread for the last three days.

Nº 2. Don't let that rat get away, put your foot on him.

Nº 3. Let him alone I'll get him.

Nº 4. Hello Sam! what are you going to do with are you going to eat them?

" 5 Certainly I am they are as good as squ make a fellows rations hold out. — go a bread and come and take dinner wil

the waters had risen and there was no hope of crossing until pontoons had been built. Lee occupied a strong position and waited for Meade's attack. Only on 12 July did the Federal army turn up in force and even then did not apply much pressure, so that Lee was able to get his whole army across the river on the night of the 13th and the following morning. Meade missed a fantastic chance to crush the defeated Confederate army and it was with an enormous sense of relief that Lee watched the last of his men cross the rickety bridge over the swollen river.

At no time in Lee's career was his strength of character better shown than in this period following the defeat at Gettysburg. He took all the blame for the battle, consoling Pickett after his repulse as we have seen, and never condemning either Ewell or Longstreet for their dilatoriness in carrying out his orders. In all his letters to his family he praises the performance of his army and explains the failure by his mistaken expectation that the soldiers could do the impossible. In a letter written to a relation who had suffered from the Federal occupation of the previous winter he apologises for his failure to remove them for good. 'I knew that crossing the Potomac would draw them off, and if we could only have been strong enough we should have detained them. But God willed otherwise, and I fear we shall soon have them all back. The army did all it could. I fear I required of it impossibilities. . . .' In front of this army he retained his composure and conducted the retreat with the calmness and confidence that the soldiers had come to expect from him, not even showing his alarm when he found himself trapped between Meade and the Potomac. All this time that he was so worried about the army he had worries of his own. He had recently heard that his wounded son Rooney had been captured at home by Federals, who later put pressure on Lee by threatening to shoot him in reprisal for some imagined Confederate wrong. Both his own wife and his daughter-in-law Charlotte were suffering from the experience of Rooney's capture – Lee's wife now confined to a wheelchair and Charlotte sickening for her terminal illness. Lee himself was not well, indeed had been sick ever since the spring, suffering from sciatica, diarrhoea and the angina pectoris which was eventually to kill him. He was getting to be too old a man to spend his life in the field and his winters in draughty tents. Yet he carried on, manoeuvring his diminished army in front of Meade, striking when Meade showed a weakness, even contemplating another invasion before he settled down for the third winter of the war behind the Rapidan. This winter was to be another cold and hungry one for the soldiers, who once again relied on religious revivals to warm their souls and log huts to warm their bodies.

It was a winter that saw movements that seemed to spell the doom of the Confederacy. Now that military affairs had taken a turn for the worse desertion became rife as soldiers disappeared into the mountains or back to homes they had not seen for over two years. Lee knew now that he would never again be strong enough to dare to cross the Potomac. The news from the west was even worse. Vicksburg had fallen to Grant on the day following Gettysburg and Federal control of the Mississippi meant that the Confederacy was now split in two. In late November the stalemate at Chattanooga was broken when 20,000 Federals charged and broke the Confederate line at Missionary Ridge, a feat as 'impossible' as Pickett's charge on 3 July. The way lay open for a Federal invasion of Georgia.

A man who could win as consistently as Ulysses S. Grant seemed manna from heaven for Lincoln in Washington. In February 1864 he was appointed general-in-chief of all the Federal armies, with greater power than any previous Federal general. He was almost unknown in Washington and when he arrived to make his first visit to Lincoln he passed unrecognised through the streets. A short, dark-haired man of forty-two with piercing eyes and a grizzled, close-cut beard, Grant had a reputation for drunkenness, as well as for the ruthlessness and tenacity which he was so soon to demonstrate to Lee in Virginia.

By early April Grant, having rejected many other plans, had made a decision on how he was going to win the war. In Virginia, Meade, under Grant's direct supervision, was to launch an army of 140,000 men against Lee and the 60,000 remaining men of the Army of Northern Virginia, pursuing him and bringing him continuously to battle until he was annihilated. In the west, Grant's red-headed lieutenant Sherman was to lead another great army against the Confederates, now led by Joe Johnston who had recovered from the wound which first gave Lee command. Once Johnston was beaten Sherman was to sweep through Georgia to the coast, destroying and burning as he went, and then if necessary join Grant to give Lee the *coup de grâce*. The whole

Hand-to-hand fighting in the
woods. (Library of Congress)

business should be over before the presidential elections in
November. And indeed there would have been few book-
makers who would have given any odds that the war would
last another winter. Things did not look too good for the
Confederacy.

168

…th between the Brooklyn 14th and 300 Rebel Cavalry

7
Long Road
to
Appomattox

THE SNOWS MELTED, the wind and the sun dried up the muddy roads and spring came to Virginia, the spring of 1864, fourth year of the terrible war. Like two great animals, the Armies of the Potomac and Northern Virginia came out of hibernation and braced themselves for their next campaign – for death or glory. North of the Rapidan were the boys in blue, dressed and fed by the greatest military supply system the world had ever seen. To the south was the world's most famous army, half-starved and dressed in rags, Lee's 'Miserables' as one who knew his Victor Hugo called them, Lee's dear soldiers – last hope of a dying cause. Many indeed had given up hope that winter, creeping off to the mountains or over to the enemy's lines, swapping pride for a full belly and a blue coat. But the others, why did they go on fighting? Could they really still dream of independence? Or were they past dreaming? They were all soldiers now. Cotton planter and squirrel hunter, dirt farmer and college boy, were all reduced to one – a man with a gun in his hand whose mental horizons were shrinking with the Confederacy. The next meal, the next billet, the next battle were all that mattered now. What was the Confederacy? Just an illusion, an idea. If they fought for anything they fought for one man who personified the Cause, a grey-haired, grey-clad man on a grey horse – Robert E. Lee, the god of war, or Uncle Bob, a more homely personification of the same man. Where Lee went, Lee's army would follow, 'one body dominated by one great inspiring soul'.

There was no pride in the man who could inspire such deep devotion. Proud he looked but humble he remained, humble before God, saddened by the condition of his men and sickened by the state of his native land. But there was to be little time for regret or tears. He had before him now a man as strong as himself, 'an ordinary scrubby-looking man with a slightly seedy look', neither a god nor an uncle but a man of terrifying simplicity, so simple that he had to win in the end. 'The art of war', said Grant, 'is simple enough. Find out where your enemy is. Get at him as soon as you can. Strike him as hard as you can and as often as you can, and keep moving on.' What could anyone do with a man who really believed that and had the moral courage and the ruthlessness to carry it out? Colonel Taylor of Lee's staff succinctly explained Grant's brutal arithmetic. 'If 140,000 men are made to grapple in a death struggle with 60,000 men; of the

PREVIOUS PAGES Confederate fortifications at Petersburg, with *chevaux-de-frise* beyond. (Brady Collection, Library of Congress)

OPPOSITE General Ulysses S. Grant, whose policy of attrition brought victory to the North. (Radio Times Hulton Picture Library)

former, 20,000 should survive the total annihilation of the latter, even though the price exacted for such destruction be in the ratio of two to one.' Lee was to inflict casualties on Grant that would have had a McClellan or a Hooker scuttling for the lines at Washington, but Grant just came on. After he crossed the Rapidan in early May someone reported to him that the pontoons had been lost. Grant was not worried. 'If I beat General Lee I sha'n't want any pontoons; and if General Lee beats me I can take all the men I intend to take back across the river on a log.'

On 4 and 5 May 1864 Grant launched four armies against the Confederacy. Across the mountains Sherman moved south with 100,000 men towards Joe Johnston and Atlanta. Grant's own advance against Lee in Virginia was flanked by two other armies, Sigel advancing up the Shenandoah and Butler landing 30,000 men on the south side of the James to threaten Richmond from the rear. It was the best co-ordinated move of the war, a tribute to Lincoln's good sense in giving

The biggest gun made during the Civil War, the mortar 'Dictator', was used by the Federals in 1865. (Radio Times Hulton Picture Library)

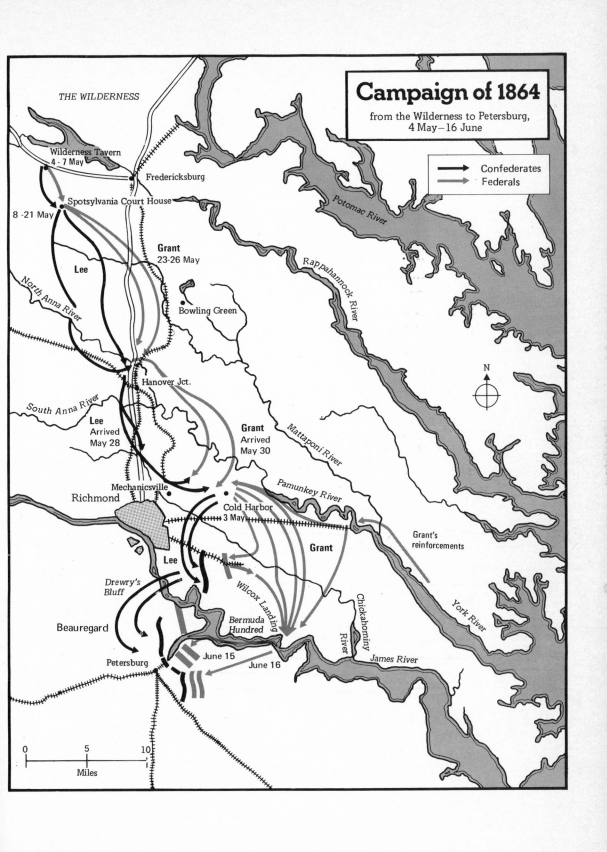

Campaign of 1864

from the Wilderness to Petersburg,
4 May–16 June

THE WILDERNESS

Wilderness Tavern
4 - 7 May

Fredericksburg

Spotsylvania Court House

8 -21 May

Lee

Grant
23-26 May

Potomac River

Rappahannock River

Confederates
Federals

North Anna River

Bowling Green

South Anna River

Hanover Jct.

Lee
Arrived
May 28

Grant
Arrived
May 30

Mattaponi River

Pamunkey River

N

Mechanicsville

Richmond

Cold Harbor
3 May

Grant

Grant's
reinforcements

Lee

York River

Drewry's
Bluff

Wilcox Landing

Chickahominy
River

Beauregard

Bermuda
Hundred

James River

Petersburg

June 15

June 16

0   5   10
Miles

Grant supreme command and a striking contrast to Lee's position. He had command only over the troops in Virginia north of Richmond and was not even able to control the defence of the city from the south, where the jealous Beauregard took pains to assert the independence of his own command, as he struggled to contain the inept Butler. Lee could do nothing but hope that Sigel and Butler would be checked, as he turned his attention to the imminent threat of Grant.

And so began the most terrible campaign of the war, Lee's attempt to stop the juggernaut. In a period of thirty days Grant and Lee fought three major battles and several minor ones, the net result of which was that Grant had moved his army some fifty miles to the south-east at a cost of some 50,000 casualties and had arrived at a place 'where he could have gone by water without losing a single man'. But this assessment misses the point. Grant had not beaten Lee but neither had Lee beaten Grant and, although Confederate casualties were well under half of those suffered by the Federals, these men were totally irreplaceable while Grant was constantly reinforced from the North. His brutal arithmetic was working.

The first clash came shortly after Grant crossed the Rapidan. Lee determined to strike him as he came through the Wilderness, in the very densest part of that twilight jungle through which Jackson had made his flank march to Chancellorsville almost exactly a year previously. Here Grant would be able to use neither his artillery nor his cavalry and Lee thought correctly that his opponent's advantage in numbers would be more than neutralised by the Southerners' knowledge of the terrain and their penchant for 'indian' fighting. Nearly everyone was agreed that the battle of the Wilderness was the most ghastly battle of the whole war. Like two animals the armies grappled in the darkness of the forest, stumbling into each other through the dense brush and swamps, attacking and counter-attacking completely blindly in this 'region of gloom and the shadow of death'. For two days the struggle went on, the forest lit up towards the end by fires which consumed the brush and the wounded, shrieking helpless beneath the trees. For years, visitors to this region were to find the skeletons of soldiers who had died in the battle and whose charred bodies were never found by friend or foe.

176

Fighting in the Wilderness, 'the region of gloom', in which the worst battle of the war was fought. (Anne S.K. Brown Military Collection)

Lee's first experience of Grant as a fighter taught him that here was a man who did not stop. The Federal advance was checked and Grant suffered terrible casualties, but he was not beaten and on the evening of 7 May he put his men on the road to the south-east to try and slip round the Confederate right and get between Lee and Richmond. It was the first of many races between the two generals. That night Anderson, commanding the corps of Longstreet who had been wounded by his own men in the battle, set out to try to beat Grant's leading corps to the important cross-roads of Spottsylvania Court House, while the cavalry checked the Federal advance. It was a close race, just won by the Confederate cavalry and Anderson so that when the main Federal army came up they found their path barred once again by the tireless rebels.

Lee was now so short of trustworthy corps commanders that he was forced to take direct tactical command of the campaign. Longstreet was wounded, Powell Hill was sick and Ewell had once again shown that he was not to be trusted to act independently. Directly he got to Spottsylvania Lee used his engineering knowledge to construct a powerful defensive position for the Federals to batter themselves to death against. Observers were astonished at the speed with which the Southerners could throw up such defences. One wrote: 'It is a rule that when the Rebels halt, the first day gives them a good rifle pit; the second a regular infantry parapet with artillery in position; and the third a parapet with an abattis in front and entrenched batteries behind. Sometimes they put this three days' work into the first twenty-four hours.' Behind these lines the fast-shooting rebels could destroy assault after assault, as they were to prove on 10 May when Grant tried to overwhelm them.

However there was one weak point in Lee's defences and both Lee and Grant had spotted it. The lines formed an inverted V with the apex facing the Federals. This apex was exposed, and Lee was preparing a new line farther back when, just before daylight on 12 May, Grant launched a massive assault. In thick fog his assault corps rushed forward with loud cheers and the Confederate division defending the salient simply disappeared. This was the worst moment of the whole campaign for Lee. His army faced the prospect of being overwhelmed by an enemy on the wrong side of their breastworks. But his soldiers still had total confidence in him. 'Marse Robert'll take care of those fellows', said one old soldier to his mate. 'He knows just what to do.' The confident assumption proved correct. Lee rushed troops in to keep the Federals from breaking completely through the line and for the rest of the day there was a savage fight for the 'Bloody Angle', in which many thousands of Lee's veterans fell before the Federals were pushed out. Once more Grant had been checked, but again his brutal arithmetic was at work.

178

Grant now took another great step to the south-east to try to outflank Lee. But Lee, like a skilful boxer who reads his opponent's mind, was there before him and this time the prepared entrenchments were too much for even Grant to contemplate attacking. There was nothing for it but to take another step to the south-east, this time landing in the swamp and pine country behind the Chickahominy where the Seven Days Battle had taken place. Grant was certainly getting nearer Richmond, but once again Lee was in front of him. One more step and Grant would find himself in the sea or the James River. Trusting that Lee's casualties in the campaign had so weakened and demoralised his army that a break-through would be possible Grant launched on 3 June one more massive assault on Lee's lines at Cold Harbor. In less than an hour Grant's drive to Richmond was finished. Seven thousand men fell before the Confederate trenches and the boys in blue had had enough. Grant called for a second assault but found no response among his men. The juggernaut had been stopped.

The hopes of the Confederacy were high in early June. Not one of Grant's four armies had succeeded. Sigel had been badly defeated by a scratch force in the Valley. The useless Butler had been bottled up and rendered ineffective by Beauregard. Johnston's skilful retreat before Sherman in the west had prevented the red-haired destroyer from getting at his opponent, and Grant had been brought to a halt in front of Richmond. Northern public opinion was shocked by the failures and sickened by Grant's casualty list. Cold Harbor had merely underlined the awful waste of the rest of the campaign. With a presidential election coming up, a war that looked as though it could never be won was bad news for the Republicans and Southern hopes were correspondingly high.

Lee was not so hopeful. Although determined to fight to the last, he was beginning to see the writing on the wall. Grant's campaign of attrition had so reduced his army that at Cold Harbor he had had not a single reserve – every man was in that line of fire which had so depressed the Northern news-papers. And what lay in the future? He no longer had the strength to do another Seven Days and drive Grant off the peninsula. Sooner or later he would be forced into the one situation he had always feared. Grant would besiege Richmond and he would have to defend it. Gone would be all chance for manoeuvre and counter-attack, and slowly starvation, desertion and Grant's big guns would do their work. Lee was also suffering from a personal grief. Jeb Stuart had been killed defending Richmond against a Federal cavalry attack. One more great leader and a great friend lost to the cause. Who was left of the great team that had won Lee's early battles? Jackson and Stuart were dead, Longstreet was wounded and Powell Hill was still sick. Now everything fell on Lee. For the last nine months of its existence he seemed to carry the whole of the Confederacy on his shoulders. Meanwhile, like a tired conjuror, he pulled an old trick out of the bag. Early was sent to the Valley to do a Jackson. He had amazing success and was soon threatening Washington, but his force was too weak to do more than threaten and in the long run Early was doomed. The net effect of this sideshow was to mean that Lee's army would be even weaker when winter came.

It was weak enough now. So weak that Lee was able to do nothing to stop Grant crossing the James in mid-June and threatening Richmond from the south. But not yet weak enough to lose Richmond. Beauregard and Lee linked up to check Grant and, by the end of the month, the war in the east had settled down to the siege of Petersburg, the railway centre some twenty miles south of Richmond and the key to the capital's continued survival. If Petersburg fell Richmond must fall.

Slowly the two lines of trenches facing each other outside Petersburg grew. Grant's aim was to force Lee to extend his line and thus to reduce his manpower per mile of trench until eventually he was so stretched that he would break. Gradually Grant pushed his trenches to the west, threatening the two railways linking Petersburg to the south and west – vital lifelines supplying food not only to Petersburg but also to Richmond. In the end Lee's lines were stretched from the Chickahominy River to the Southside Railway west of Petersburg, thirty-five miles of trenches defended by barely 1,000 men to the mile facing three times that number in the Federal lines. Lee was everywhere, making full use of the knowledge gained in a lifetime of engineering and at the same time raising morale by his very appearance. Siege warfare hardly suited that panache which was the Confederate strength, but the soldiers kept at it right through' the long cold wet winter of 1864-5. Weak with hunger, anaemic and

Ball of 2nd Corps. Washington Bulding. Feb 22. 1864

While Richmond approached starvation the Federal forces in Washington relaxed at splendid balls. (Library of Congress)

OPPOSITE William Tecumseh Sherman, famed for his destructive march from Atlanta through Georgia to the sea. (Bettmann Archive)
ABOVE Even the railroad tracks were ripped up and melted to make them useless. (Library of Congress)

depressed, they often had to dig in ground frozen a foot deep as they struggled to extend and strengthen the defences. Meanwhile Grant was not idle. The Confederates were kept close to exhaustion by his pendulum threats to their line, first out to the west, then north of the James, sometimes in both places at once. Lee rushed men from place to place and the line held.

Inside the lines life went on for the war-weary population of the two cities. Supplies were never completely cut off and Richmond never reached that state of total starvation which has so often been the fate of besieged cities. But starvation was approaching as the Federal stranglehold tightened and the hopes of early June slowly disappeared. Early was defeated in the Valley and Sheridan, Grant's very successful cavalry commander, proceeded to turn Virginia's bread-basket into a desert. Jefferson Davis, fed up with Joe Johnston's well-managed retreat before Sherman, replaced him by the

pugnacious Hood. Hood, promoted to fight, went out and fought, lost the battle and lost Atlanta. The way was open to Georgia. Sherman left behind part of his army under Thomas to deal with any further activity on the part of Hood and then set off with 60,000 men on his famous march from Atlanta to the sea. Marching on a front forty miles wide and virtually unresisted, he swept the country clean, living off the land and burning and destroying all that he did not need. He reached the sea in mid-December and by the 22nd had captured the sea-port of Savannah and was ready to turn north to link up with Grant. One week earlier Thomas had completely routed Hood at Nashville and the Confederates now no longer had an army in the west.

Indeed there was not much of a Confederacy left. The once proud state was now confined to the virtually independent region of Texas and the area south of Richmond comprising southern Virginia and the Carolinas. Ready to move into this area were Sheridan in the Valley, Sherman in Georgia and Thomas in Tennessee, while Grant hammered away at the gates of Petersburg. In the middle of January 1865 Wilmington, North Carolina, fell – the last port through which blockade runners were able to supply the Confederacy – and the encirclement was complete. At this late moment Jefferson Davis decided to appoint Lee commander-in-chief of the Confederate armies, a position which he was able to hold for just two months.

While Confederate hopes collapsed in the west and in the Valley, Lee struggled on to maintain the defences of Petersburg against Grant. But the situation was rapidly becoming untenable. At the same time as Grant forced him to extend his lines the available manpower to hold them was declining. Death, disease and desertion in the ranks was continuous through the long winter and there was no one who could replace the vanished veterans. Lee and Davis tried everything. Civilians were summarily impressed and marched to the front but most deserted almost immediately. Old men, boys and walking wounded found themselves in the lines. But it was no good; the defence was still too thin. There was one last resort. The Negroes must be armed and taken into the army. Lee's argument was quite logical. If we lose there will be no more slavery. If we do not have more men then we will lose. We have no option but to arm the Negroes in return for the promise of emancipation. Such an idea took some swallowing in the Confederate Congress, but respect for Lee saw the measure passed, too late however for it to be put into practice. But the very fact that Congress was prepared to accept emancipation of the slaves as the price of independence is an interesting comment on Southern motivation in the war.

Lee knew by early 1865 that he could not hold Petersburg much longer. One day Grant's men would break his line. There was only one thing he could do – abandon the capital and link up with the only remaining force in the Confederacy, the army composed of soldiers from the Carolinas and the remnants of Hood's routed troops, now commanded once again by Joe Johnston. It was just possible (in a beautiful world where everything went right) that Lee and Johnston together could defeat Sherman, now moving north through South Carolina, and then turn round to defeat Grant. Since nobody was prepared to surrender while there was still hope, however faint, this was what Lee planned to do.

If Lee wanted to join Johnston he had to get out to the south-west past the left-flank of Grant's long line of trenches. In order to get the time and space to do this he planned to attack Grant's right, hoping that success would cut Grant's supply lines and force him to bring back men from the left to protect his right. In 1862 or 1863 such a plan might have worked, but not in 1865 and not against Grant. What in fact

The view of Petersburg and its suburbs from Lee's headquarters. (Radio Times Hulton Picture Library)

happened was exactly the opposite. Lee's attack on Grant's
right after an early success failed and he lost 5,000 valuable
men. Meanwhile Grant prepared an attack on Lee's right and
forced him to draw men from his thinly held trenches to try
and check him. On 1 April Sheridan, now back with his
cavalry after destroying the Shenandoah Valley, attacked
Lee's right at the cross-roads of Five Forks. The Confederate
commander was General Pickett, hero of the great charge at
Gettysburg, but he, like so many former heroes, was to lose
his reputation in these last days of the war. When the Federals
attacked and overwhelmed his troops he and the cavalry
leader Fitz Lee were enjoying a traditional Virginian feast – a
shad bake – and by the time they had finished their meal the
battle was lost. Indeed more than just the battle had been lost.
Sheridan's capture of Five Forks barred Lee's escape route
to the south-west. Worse still, the men withdrawn to fight
for Pickett had left the rest of the trenches very thinly
manned. That afternoon Grant ordered an assault on Lee's
centre and, after a heavy bombardment, a wild rush by the
Federals at dawn on 2 April broke through Lee's trenches and
stormed onwards until they were halted by the Appomattox
River, killing Powell Hill on the way. After nine months the
siege of Petersburg was over and Lee now had no choice but
to get out west as fast as possible.

Everyone agreed that Sunday 2 April was a lovely spring

Refugees stream out of
Richmond, leaving behind a
burning city, on the night
of 2 April 1865. (Museum of
the Confederacy)

A Northern impression
of the Union army
entering Richmond through
cheering crowds.
(British Museum)

day and everyone in Richmond had gone to church to look at everybody else. One lady was looking at President Davis when he was given a slip of paper and she saw him suddenly turn pale. The note told the still optimistic President that the Petersburg line had been broken and that Richmond must be evacuated that same night. For four years the defence of Richmond had been the central idea in all Davis's thinking about the war and his determination to keep defending it had been the main reason for Lee's long delay in pulling his army out of its increasingly hopeless position. Now he had to leave. Still dreaming impossible dreams, Davis and the Confederate government left that night for the west on the only railway still linking Richmond to the outside world. They left behind them a burning city, burned by Southerners who remembered vaguely that the correct form for people evacuating a stronghold was to render it useless to the enemy. Up in flames went

The ruins of Richmond
(Brady Collection, Library
of Congress)

armouries and arsenals, tobacco warehouses and flour mills. Out of their holes came the wretched poor of the city to loot what they could while they could. Next morning the Federals marched in, put the fires out and brought some order to the hungry, looting mob. Respectable citizens did not like the saucy look of the Federal Negro troops, but found most of their captors surprisingly polite – some small consolation perhaps for the end of their hopes. Some indeed still had hope, 'a mad vain hope that Lee would yet make a stand somewhere – that Lee's dear soldiers would give us back our liberty'.

Even Lee's soldiers had hopes. The long line of men marched out along the north bank of the Appomattox River through the night. By midnight the evacuation was completed and there was silence in the trenches. Next morning, in the fine spring weather, they felt once again that pride in

189

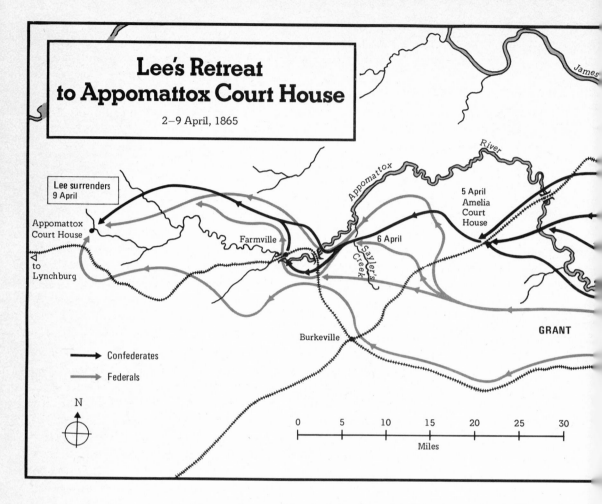

**Lee's Retreat
to Appomattox Court House**

2–9 April, 1865

James

Appomattox

River

Lee surrenders
9 April

5 April
Amelia
Court
House

Appomattox
Court House

Farmville

6 April

Sayler's Creek

to
Lynchburg

GRANT

Burkeville

→ Confederates

→ Federals

N

0   5   10   15   20   25   30

Miles

themselves and in their leader which had sustained them on so
many hard campaigns. 'Marse Robert'll take care of those
fellows. He knows just what to do.' Did he? Lee's last week as
commander of the Army of Northern Virginia was a night-
mare. Everything went wrong as he tried desperately to get
his army out of the clutches of Grant and his Federal horde.
Pickett's defeat at Five Forks had meant that there was no
chance of moving south-west towards Johnston. The only
way out was due west towards the mountains and the faint
hope that Grant would make a mistake and he could slip
through to the south.

Unfortunately for Lee, all the mistakes were to be made by
his own men, many now dispirited or frankly defeatist. The
first and most terrible check to the spirit of his army was the
discovery that someone in Richmond had failed to forward

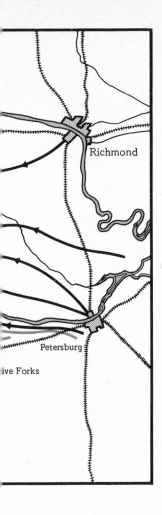

the rations to feed the men on the march. When Lee arrived at the railway station at Amelia Court House he found no supplies and his army was doomed to starvation. Foraging for food in the immediate neighbourhood brought few full stomachs and meant delay sufficient for Grant to catch up and Sheridan's cavalry with their seven-shot repeating rifles to overtake the Confederate retreat and bar their way to the south.

Lee marched on to the west, but his army shrank hourly as men fell out famished by the roadside or simply disappeared, giving up, hoping to find their long way back to their families. On 6 April Lee's rearguard, led by Ewell and composed of some of the toughest of his veterans, was swallowed up with little effort by the Federal vanguard at Sayler's Creek. Now Lee had only some 10,000 men left and these were being picked off by Sheridan's troopers as they staggered towards the sunset. That night Lee found two days' rations in the small town of Farmville, two days' rations to get him to Appomattox Court House, last hope and last supply depot to the west. If he could beat Grant there he might . . . If, if, if.

Late in the afternoon of the following day Lee received a note from Grant demanding his surrender. He replied asking for terms. They were simple – lay down your arms. Lee prevaricated. 'To be frank, I do not think the emergency has arisen to call for the surrender of this army.' That emergency was soon to come. By the evening of the 8th, Lee had learned that Sheridan had beaten him in the race to Appomattox Court House and had captured his stores. Lee consulted with his remaining generals and it was decided to make one last attempt to break through in the morning. At 3 am the Confederates moved forward for the last time, reaching the heights a little beyond the Court House at dawn. Daylight revealed the way barred by Sheridan's troopers. Southern guns and horsemen forced Sheridan's line to open up, only to reveal beyond them two corps of Federal infantry. Lee was surrounded. There were many who would have been happy to scatter individually with their guns, to carry on a bitter guerrilla warfare in the hills. But Lee would not condemn the South to the results of this, to an everlasting bitterness and hate. There were many who would have preferred death to surrender, but there were others to think of too. 'It is our duty to live', said Lee. 'What will become of the women and children of the South if we are not here to protect them?' Lee

OPPOSITE ABOVE The first
day of Gettysburg,
painted by James Walker.
(West Point Museum
Collections, U.S.
Military Academy)

BELOW 'A Skirmish in the
Wilderness' by Winslow
Homer. (The New Britain
Museum of American Art,
New Britain, Connecticut.
Harriet Russell
Stanley Fund)

knew his duty, even if his heart was breaking, and he sent in a
flag of truce. The Federal commanders gave the order to
cease fire.

Lee went into his tent and donned his best uniform and
sword. About eleven o'clock, accompanied only by Colonel
Marshall of his staff, he rode through his lines to meet Grant
at the house of a Mr McLean. Grant, riding straight in from
the field in an old uniform, made a striking contrast to his
immaculate enemy. But even if he was not such a gentleman
as the patrician who stood before him, he was gentleman
enough not to rejoice at the downfall of his foe. Sensitive to
the elder man's pride, he tried to put him at his ease by dis-
cussing friends they had in common in the old army. Lee,
struggling to control his emotions, brought him to the point.
What were the terms of surrender?

Grant had discussed this question with Lincoln and
Sherman at the end of March. All had agreed that the peace
should be easy and that there should be no reprisals. The
sooner the soldiers went home and took up peaceful
occupations, the sooner could the horrors of the war be
forgotten and something approaching a normal life replace
the four years of bloodletting. With this in mind, Grant's
terms were astonishingly generous. Lee's soldiers were to lay
down their arms and return to their homes, the officers to
keep their swords and those cavalrymen and gunners who
owned their horses to take them home with them for the
spring ploughing. On learning that Lee's men were without
rations he agreed to supply them out of the abundant Federal
stores. Grant's generosity took some of the sting out of defeat
and Lee was appreciative. 'This will have a very happy effect
upon my army', he said.

After signing the papers Lee rode sadly back to his lines,
head bare and tears streaming down his cheeks. When the
men saw their leader their first instinct was to give a great
cheer, then there was silence as the reality of what had
happened sank in. The 'deathless' Army of Northern
Virginia had surrendered and it was all over. No one blamed
Lee. He had done all he could, and on that last unthinkable
day the tired and careworn general was regarded with more
sincere affection by his tear-stained, sunburned veterans than
ever before.

Lee's last duty to his army was to prepare a farewell
message, the famous General Order No. 9, explaining his

OVERLEAF Lee surrenders to
Grant at Appomattox Court
House. (U.S. National
Park Service)

192

'Furling the Flags' by
R. Brooke (West Point
Museum Collections,
U.S. Military Academy)

reasons for surrender and expressing his gratitude for the
loyalty of his courageous men.

After four years of arduous service, marked by unsurpassed
courage and fortitude, the Army of Northern Virginia has been
compelled to yield to overwhelming numbers and resources. I
need not tell the brave survivors of so many hard fought battles,
who have remained steadfast to the last, that I have consented to
this result from no distrust of them. But feeling that valor and
devotion could accomplish nothing that would compensate for the
loss that would have attended the continuance of the contest, I
determined to avoid the useless sacrifice of those whose past
services have endeared them to their countrymen. By the terms of

Robert E. Lee

Head Quarters Army of Northern Va.
10th Apl. 1865 -

General Order
No. 9

After four years of arduous service marked by unsurpassed courage and fortitude, the Army of Northern Virginia has been compelled to yield to overwhelming numbers and resources.

I need not tell the brave survivors of so many hard fought battles, who have remained steadfast to the last, that I have consented to this result from no distrust of them.

But feeling that valor and devotion could accomplish nothing that would compensate for the loss that would have attended the continuance of the contest, I determined to avoid the useless sacrifice of those whose past services have endeared them to their countrymen.

By the terms of the agreement officers and men can return to their homes and remain until exchanged. You will take with you the satisfaction that proceeds from the consciousness of duty faithfully performed, and I earnestly pray that a Merciful God will extend to you his blessing and protection.

With an unceasing admiration of your constancy and devotion to your Country and a grateful remembrance of your kind and generous consideration for myself, I bid you all an affectionate farewell -

R. E. Lee
Genl.

The farewell address,
General Order No. 9, from
Lee to his army.
(The Bettmann Archive)

the agreement officers and men can return to their homes and remain until exchanged. You will take with you the satisfaction that proceeds from the consciousness of duty faithfully performed, and I earnestly pray that a Merciful God will extend to you His blessing and protection. With an increasing admiration of your constancy and devotion to your country, and a grateful remembrance of your kind and generous consideration for myself, I bid you all an affectionate farewell.

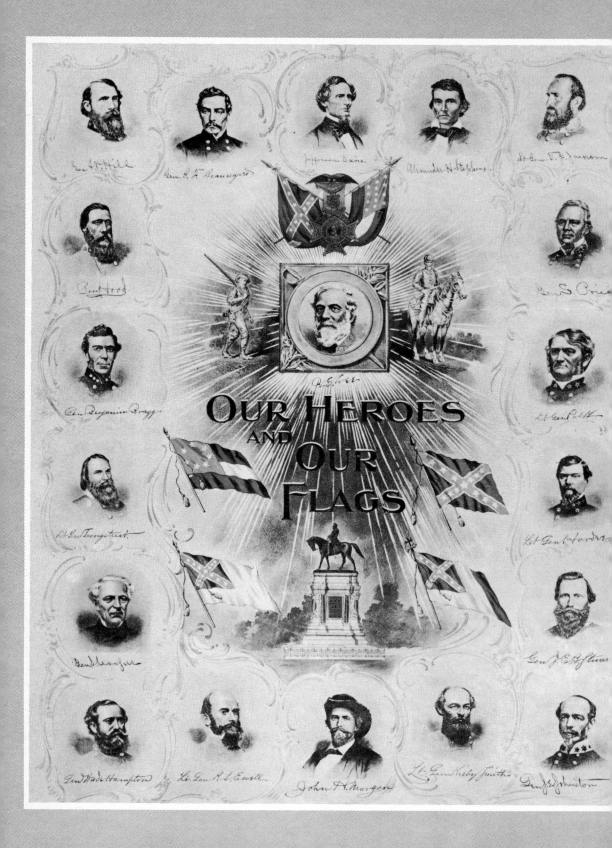

OUR HEROES
AND
OUR FLAGS

8
Birth of a Legend

W HEN THE SAD AND DEFEATED Robert E. Lee rode away from his army he rode out of most people's history and into legend. The man who had done his duty, as he saw it, by resigning from the United States Army and fighting for his native state had become a saint. The South needed a saint after the rigours of the war; a saint whose nobility and courage could furnish the best proof that the cause had been a worthy one and the young men of the South had not died in vain. Some would go further and compare Lee's surrender to the crucifixion, the culminating sacrifice at the end of his long road to Appomattox. Lee himself told his staff, as he rode out to meet Grant, that he would rather die a thousand deaths than face what he then had to face. Others change the image and think of Lee as another Owen Glendower, an elderly warrior living in the mountains with his faithful band of followers, waiting for another day to sally forth against the Federals.

Lee was not crucified nor did he hide in the mountains. What he did do was both harder and more useful to his shattered people who looked to him for an example in this time of despair. He determined to stay in Virginia and do all that he could to promote a new harmony between the severed parts of the now restored Union. Once defeated he accepted the arbitration of war and begged all Southerners to do the same. But to accept Federal rule was more than some could bear. Many Confederates went abroad. Men from the Army of Texas marched across the border to offer their services to the Emperor of Mexico. Others stayed at home but never became reconciled to defeat, living out their bitter lives in harsh condemnation of that fate which had doomed them to failure. Lee's own gospel was a simple one, adopted by that great majority of Southerners who still saw him as their leader. It was a gospel of silence, goodwill, patience and hard work.

Silence was necessary if memories of the war were not to call forth recriminations which would mean no hope of harmony between the sections. Lee rarely talked of the war in the five years of life remaining to him, though the memory of it was constantly with him. Day after day he would be reminded of it as veterans rushed up to clasp his hand, as tourists from the North begged for one glimpse of the 'rebel chieftain' and as crowds formed wherever he went to cheer the incarnation of their failed hopes. Lee acknowledged this

PREVIOUS PAGES Lee surrounded by the Confederate heroes. (Library of Congress)

200

Richmond ladies going to receive government rations, with the caption 'Don't you think that Yankee must feel like shrinking into his boots before such high-toned Southern ladies as we?' (British Museum)

respect and admiration, but would not be drawn out on the war or on the present condition of his people. Only in one respect did he outwardly show interest in those four crowded years. He was determined that history should know the odds against which he and his men had been fighting. At one time he thought of writing the history of the war himself and, when he abandoned this idea, he encouraged others to tell the truth about his campaigns.

Harder than silence was goodwill and patience in the face of the adversities which 'Reconstruction' brought to the South. The day that Lee rode into Richmond from Appomattox was the day that Abraham Lincoln was assassinated at Ford's Theatre in Washington. Lincoln's death meant the end of any hopes of an easy peace and rapid assimilation of the erring states into the Union. His successor Andrew Johnson tried hard to fulfil Lincoln's policy, and the South was ready to accept defeat and repudiate both secession and slavery, the

two principles on which the war had been fought. But the
Radical Republicans controlled Congress, and were able to
replace Johnson's easy peace by a much more vindictive
policy in which the South was treated as a conquered land.
The era of the 'carpetbaggers' had begun. The South was to
be ruled by military governors and her legislative assemblies
were to be elected on a franchise which was open to Negroes,
but not to white men who had been associated in any way with
the government or the armies of the Confederacy. The
corruption and humiliation that followed in the next decade
was hard for the proud Southerners to bear, and it was in
these conditions that such institutions as the Ku Klux Klan
sprang up as a sign of continued Southern defiance. Lee kept
out of politics and deprecated violence, advocating goodwill
towards that strong body of public opinion in the North
opposed to the excesses of the Radicals and patience while
that public opinion had its effect. He lived long enough to see
Virginia restored as a state of the Union in 1870, one of the
first of the Southern states to have a government free of
carpetbaggers and dominated by white conservatives. Later
in the century all Southern states were to have such govern-
ments and the Negroes were to be abandoned by the North
as readily as their cause had been taken up during Reconstruction in order to provide docile voters for the vindictive
policies of the Radical Republicans.

Hard work – the fourth item in Lee's gospel – was the most
necessary of all. The type of warfare advocated by Pope and
put into practice by such generals as Sherman and Sheridan
had turned the once rich section into a ravaged land. Fields
had been left untilled, houses and barns burned, stock run
off or slaughtered, irrigation systems destroyed and the labour
force dispersed or killed. It is estimated that over quarter of
a million Southerners were lost in action, from wounds, or
through disease in the course of the war – nearly five per cent
of the entire white population and well over a quarter of the
numbers put into the field. On top of this the planters and
farmers faced the dispersal of the former Negro slaves. They
had scattered throughout the Union; many had abandoned
the land and were congregated in cities where they often
lived on Federal hand-outs. Both in town and country the
Negroes found it difficult to acclimatise to the habit of paid
work and to the bitter discovery that prejudice was as strong
after the war as before it.

Southerners, both black and white, had to adapt to the new situation. In the long run there was no alternative solution to hard work, to a struggle to get a crop in 1865 and then to put talents and work together to provide a living in the future. Many a former planter and patrician found himself working what remained of his land with his own labour, as did Lee's sons, Rooney and Rob. But many others had no land, or had lost the will and determination to hold down a civilian job during the long years in the army. One of the saddest sights for Lee was to see his once proud veterans destitute and idle in a world that now had no use for their particular talents.

Lee himself was not treated badly after his surrender, though it was to be three years before his status became clarified. His first need was for a long period of rest and recuperation after the strain of the last months of the war. During this period he was officially a paroled prisoner-of-war. By a proclamation of 29 May, amnesty and pardon were offered to all Confederates who would take an oath supporting the Constitution and laws of the United States. However, senior officers like Lee were exempted from this general offer and were required to make an individual application to the President. Lee, anxious to remove all grounds for bitterness now the war was over, was determined to set an example by accepting the authority of the Federal government and applied for the pardon. He received no reply. Meanwhile a Federal grand jury had indicted him for treason on 7 June. He was never tried and the case lapsed. Eventually he was included in the General Pardon of Christmas 1868, though he never recovered the property which had been seized during the war. Altogether the Northerners showed remarkable leniency towards the Southern leaders, only marred by the long imprisonment without trial of Jefferson Davis.

Long before he was pardoned Lee had recovered from the physical strains of the war and was considering in what way he should fulfil his own gospel of hard work. His first inclinations were towards farming. But then in August 1865 he received a totally unexpected offer to take up the Presidency of a run-down college – Washington College at Lexington in the Valley of Virginia. Lee accepted and, for the rest of his life, he took this opportunity to try and instil some of his own principles into the students who flocked from all over the Union to a college run by such a famous man. It is difficult

OPPOSITE 'Lee's Farewell' by R.H.Pine. (Washington and Lee University)

The chapel built under Lee's directions in 1867, in which he and his family are buried. (Washington and Lee University)

RIGHT A political cartoon caricaturing Andrew Johnson as Iago to a Negro Othello, from *Harper's Weekly*, 1866. (Phoebus Picture Library)

to think of a better way in which the non-political Lee could have influenced the future of his country than by demonstrating to the students, many of them war veterans, the arts of peace and the importance of an end to hate. His name attracted money from Northern industrialists and philanthropists which was used to build up more modern studies, especially the sciences, whilst his influence and personality were able to check the natural tendency of the Southern students to demonstrate against the more outrageous aspects of military and carpetbagger rule.

RADICAL RIOTS

WHAT THEY WERE.

ANDREW JOHNSON'S RECONSTRUCTION,

TREASON IS A CRIME AND MUST BE MADE ODIOUS, AND TRAITORS MUST BE PUNISHED.

LOVE THINE ENEMIES

I AM YOUR MOSES

PARDON TO REBELS

VETOES TO UNION MEN

OTHELLO. DOST THOU MOCK ME?
IAGO.   I MOCK YOU! NO, BY HEAVEN:
WOULD YOU WOULD BEAR YOUR FORTUNES LIKE A MAN. *SHAKSPEARE.*

1862.

1866.

HOW IT WORKS. *Th. Nast.*

ABOVE Lee in his study at
Washington College, by
A. J. Volck from sketches
made from life.
(Valentine Museum)

Lee's wife Mary in old age.
(Virginia Historical Society)

Lee was able to enjoy in Lexington the longest period of uninterrupted family life since his marriage. He seemed happy at home, looking after his invalid wife and his three surviving daughters. Sixty years old in 1867, he remained the noble patriarch to the outside world, an object of pilgrimage and veneration. But there was a hint of sadness in his mouth and slowly he began to lose the magnificent carriage of his prime. Sometimes he seemed to be restless and he often went for long rides by himself in the countryside on his faithful grey war-horse, Traveller, who had carried him through his campaigns. By 1869 he was troubled with rheumatism and a return of the old heart trouble which had bothered him in the year of Gettysburg.

His doctor and his colleagues at the college urged him to go south in early 1870 to seek the sun for the benefit of his health. The tour proved to be a triumphal progress through Georgia and the Carolinas which did little to improve his health, but demonstrated the continued love and veneration felt for the now ageing man by the people of the South. Back in Virginia he gradually declined and died at home in Lexington on 12 October. In his last days his mind seemed to be on the war. 'Tell Hill he must come up', he said distinctly in the midst of some incoherent muttering, thinking perhaps of Sharpsburg where the late arrival of A.P.Hill saved the day. His last words have a military meaning, but he could well have been thinking of a non-military journey when he called out, 'strike the tent'.

The Old South was fortunate in the men who wrote its epitaph. A civilisation whose death agonies were attended by men such as Lee, Jackson and Jeb Stuart was a civilisation that would never really die. The sons and grandsons of the men who rode through Georgia and the Carolinas to die on the battlefields of Virginia were to remember proudly the deeds of their forefathers, as they struggled to cope with a world in which slave and plantation, honour and gentility had no place. The South which Lee pledged to silence still had its dreams; dreams of glory and dreams of a vanished life-style very different from the harsh reality of the ante-bellum world. This glory and this imagined life-style were to be enshrined in scores of novels and memoirs as the century went on, until today we have two Old Souths, one real and one pure myth.

Robert E.Lee fits into both these pictures, half man, half myth. His biographer starts off by thinking that no man could be so good and noble as the myth suggests he was. How could anyone maintain such a high standard of behaviour through a lifetime? But the more one reads the more one realises that for the most part the myth is true. Robert E.Lee really was like that. Born into the blue blood of Virginia, bred to be great and good, he retained his self control and self confidence all his life to emerge as the right man at the right moment to make Southern dreams of independence more than a mere mockery.

210

The funeral cortege of
Robert E. Lee turning into
the main street of
Lexington. (Washington
and Lee University)

As a soldier he clearly had faults, most of them the result of his virtues. He was too affable and too kind to be a totally effective military leader. By refusing to assert his full authority over his generals he jeopardised more than one of his campaigns. Even more serious was his failure as a quarter-master. That picturesque appearance of the Army of Northern Virginia, those rags, those empty bellies, must be blamed in part at least on Lee. Since he never bullied Richmond for supplies he never got them. He begged and pleaded but only bullying could have brought order out of Southern chaos. And so time after time his campaigns were dictated by subsistence rather than strategy. A man like McClellan won the love of his troops by feeding them well. Lee also won the love of his troops but he had to do it in a different way.

What was the magic which could make Lee's horde of ragamuffins such a fantastic fighting machine under his command and still keep them together when disaster threatened? Much of the magic lay in the men themselves. Observers were astonished at the courage and individual fighting skills of the Confederate soldier, whoever commanded them. But Lee was to do more. Somehow he changed these individualists into a machine; a machine which followed him but never lost the individuality of its parts. Much of his leadership depended on his mere physical appearance. The sight of the magnificent but simply dressed Lee on his horse at a moment of crisis was often enough to change defeat into victory. Lee realised this and there are innumerable instances of him riding up to the front when his soldiers were hard-pressed. Then the soldiers would cheer and refuse to attack until their beloved leader had retired out of danger. They liked to know that their Apollo was as brave as they were, but they had no wish to see him killed.

Simplicity as well as magnificence was part of Lee's magic. Although he always kept a certain distance from his men, he shared their lives. His uniforms were never flashy, he slept on the ground like they did, he ate the same food and endured the same hardships. The continuous stream of parcels of delicacies and clothing that arrived at headquarters from his civilian admirers were distributed to the soldiers. Such informality was necessary to win the affection and respect of an army of citizen soldiers who were more inclined to follow a superior man than an established authority. Not that it should be thought that Lee was soft. He could be a firmer disciplinarian than most civil war generals, as many recaptured deserters found to their cost. Offenders must be punished, even executed he said, 'unless some reason be presented which will enable me to be lenient without creating a bad precedent, and encouraging others to be offenders'. Lee's discipline was stern but fair and was seen to be just.

None of Lee's characteristics as a general and as a man would have been of much value to the South if he had not been so often a winner. Up to Gettysburg, indeed right up to the siege of Petersburg, the soldiers and civilians of the South had a fixed and unshakeable faith in all he did and a calm confidence of victory when serving under him. Lee knew what to do, and the astonishing audacity of some of his battle plans only increased this total belief in his ability. Military historians have criticised Lee for dividing his outnumbered army in the face of the enemy at such great battles as the Seven Days, Second Bull Run and Chancellorsville. The only sensible answer to such criticism is that Lee won all these battles. Others have said that Lee did well only because of the incompetence of those opposed to him. There is obviously much truth in this, and some of Lee's greatest victories were won because he could read so clearly the minds of lesser men, such as McClellan, Pope and Hooker. But this need not deter too much from his reputation. A man needs to have something on his side when he consistently fights battles against an enemy with twice his numbers.

Could the South ever have won? Such hypothetical questions are as fascinating as they are useless. The South did not win, and with hindsight it is difficult to see how they ever could have, given the resolution of Lincoln and the Radicals and the industrial and military power of the North. But sometimes one wonders. Sometimes total victory seemed so close. What would have happened if Lee had been able to follow up some of his battles and capture whole armies, as when McClellan was huddled by the riverside at Harrison's Landing or Hooker was fleeing back across the Rappahannock? What would have happened if the three cigars had not been left behind at Frederick, Maryland in 1862 or if Stuart had not got separated from the army on the Gettysburg Campaign? Southerners love to ask these questions but of course they have no answer. After Gettysburg victory seemed impossible and Lee won no more decisive battles, but the war went on for another twenty-one months. What kept the South going? It is difficult for us today to believe that many could have felt that independence was then still possible. But they obviously did. And why? Because they still thought that Lee could perform miracles, as indeed he did in his 1864 campaign. He had become superhuman, able to do the impossible. Such beliefs survived the war and entered into myth. Lee the great soldier had become a saint and more than a saint. As a young lady said when she saw him in the year of his death, 'We have heard of God, but here was General Lee!'

Lee on his favourite horse, Traveller. (The Virginia Historical Society)

Select Bibliography

There are innumerable books on Lee and the Civil War in existence. These below are just those which I found to be most useful when writing this book. A weighty and fairly reliable background to the whole period is by J.G.Randall, *The Civil War and Reconstruction* (1937). A good short introduction to the subject is Winston S.Churchill's *The American Civil War* (1958). My favourite amongst the many full-length narrative histories were the three volumes of the Centennial History of the Civil War by Bruce Catton, *The Coming Fury* (1961), *Terrible Swift Sword* (1963) and *Never Call Retreat* (1965).

The classic biography of Lee is by Douglas Southall Freeman, *R.E.Lee*, 4 vols. (1934-5), abridged into one volume by Richard Harwell (1961). Two early studies by members of his staff are very useful: Walter H.Taylor, *Four Years with General Lee* (1877) and A.L.Long, *Memoirs of R.E.Lee* (1886). Best of all is the recent biography by Clifford Dowdey, *Lee* (1970).

Two collections of documents give much insight into Lee and the period as a whole: *The Wartime Papers of R.E.Lee*, edited by Clifford Dowdey and Louis H.Manarin (1961) and *The Blue and the Gray*, edited by Henry S.Commager, 2 vols. (1950).

On soldier life in the Confederate Army the best summary is by Bell Irwin Wiley, *The Life of Johnny Reb* (1943). Of the numerous memoirs I preferred Carlton McCarthy, *Detailed Minutiae of Soldier Life in the Army of Northern Virginia* (1882) and Robert Stiles, *Four Years under Marse Robert* (1903).

Other useful memoirs and diaries giving a good idea of life in the Confederacy include William Howard Russell, *My Diary North and South* (1863); Arthur J.L.Fremantle, *Three Months in the Southern States* (1864); J.B.Jones, *A Rebel War Clerk's Diary*, 2 vols. (1935); Mary Boykin

Chesnut, *A Diary from Dixie* (new ed. 1949) and Judith McGuire, *Diary of a Southern Refugee* (1868).

The classic account of Lee's main opponents is William Swinton, *Campaigns of the Army of the Potomac* (1866). See also Ulysses S. Grant, *Personal Memoirs*, 2 vols. (1885).

Index